AN ANTONINE

CAMERON BLACK

DITCH, BERM, RAMPART – WEST OF WATLING LODGE

Over 70 colour illustrations, including 8 large-scale day-walk maps

For the Cramond Walkers

AN ANTONINE TRAIL

A Roaming Holiday: On Foot from Clyde to Forth
124.5 km or 77 miles

CAMERON BLACK

Copyright: © Cameron Black 2014

Published by Cameron Black
Web-site: www.waysandtrails.co.uk
Email: contact@waysandtrails.co.uk

Copyright: © Cameron Black 2014
The text and photographs are by Cameron Black
Front cover photo 'Roger Barr on Bar Hill'
Back cover photo 'Entrance to Auld Kirk Museum, Kirkintilloch'

The mapping is by David Langworth
(E-mail: david@maps.myzen.co.uk)
It is reproduced by permission of Ordinance Survey
on behalf of HMSO. © Crown copyright 2014
All rights reserved. Licence number 100050107

ISBN: 978-0-9566500-1-6

Previously work by Cameron Black includes:

THE SAINT ANDREW'S WAY
The modern restoration of a medieval pilgrimage walk
from central Edinburgh across the Forth Road Bridge to St Andrews
ISBN: 978-0-9566500-0-9

FOREWORD

*By Professor David J Breeze OBE, FSA, FRSE,
Former Chief Inspector of Ancient Monuments for Scotland,
Past President of the Society of Antiquaries of Scotland.*

The Antonine Wall has long lived under the shadow of its southern neighbour, Hadrian's Wall. Yet, at the time of its construction, the Antonine Wall was the most advanced frontier design in the Roman Empire. Its misfortune is to have been built in turf and timber rather than stone. It has therefore suffered rather more from the ravages of time than Hadrian's Wall. In spite of the Industrial Revolution, the Agricultural Revolution and the resulting explosion in the population of Scotland, there is more of the Wall to see than is generally realised. This is partly because there are few long stretches to walk and much is hidden in woods and the corners of housing estates.

Accordingly, I warmly welcome the publication of Cameron Black's detailed guide for walkers along the Antonine Wall. It will be indispensable for those wishing to explore Rome's north-west frontier which is also Scotland's newest World Heritage Site.

David J Breeze

ACKNOWLEDGEMENTS

I have found it easier to uncover what the Romans did in 142 AD in the vicinity of the Antonine Wall, than to discover what our present-day inhabitants do. Here are snippets from but two conversations I have had:

    1) In Kirkintilloch, I asked if anyone ever tried to walk along the line of the Wall.
    "Oh yes," came the reply, "many have done it. It can be done in three days, two even: and there are books about it!"
    2) In Castlecary, where a 'Roman' gate has been erected to mark the Best Wall Walk, I asked if many folk were passing through.
    "Oh no, no one at all ever does that."

I think the truth of the matter will have to rely on *you*. So, thank *you* and do enjoy our Trail. I also thank David Langworth for his excellent walking maps. Barry Cross offered valuable criticism of my text ("I have no idea what you mean, here") and he highlighted suspect passages for me with sound advice. Callum Black, as had Barry, attempted a desk study to follow the route: I took on board his wise remarks. Dr Gillian Black, Senior Lecturer in Law at the University of Edinburgh, has done her best to keep me out of court and tells me where to insert a comma in line 27. Gavin and Donald Black helped design the book's layout. Andrew Johnson, restoring his medieval tower-house of Castle Cary, showed me some Roman stones in its walls. Peter Yeoman, Head of Cultural Heritage for Historic Scotland, and who provided background to my earlier book "The Saint Andrew's Way", kindly and bravely put me in touch with David Breeze who *also* marked my work and saved me from embarrassment by correcting various errors – telling me who Constantine was and what the Venerable Bede thought – and keeping me on the straight and narrow, helpful when following a Trail. He has also, obligingly, penned a Foreword for you. Iain and Anne Hendrie have gone further than most: they have actually checked the route on the ground with me. Roger Barr and Harry MacPhail checked the Trail on sunny days, using trains.

    My thanks to them all.

CONTENTS

Acknowledgements	6
Preamble & Pretext	8
Introduction	10
An Antonine Trail: Map	14
Distances	15

PART ONE: ROMAN — 17

1) Veni, Vidi, Vici	18
2) Its a Date and Other Numbers	19
3) Seven is a Big Number	22
4) Rewards from Rome	25
5) Chronology was the problem	33
6) About the Antonine Wall	34
7) What happened next?	37
8) If the Romans had had a Forth & Clyde Canal	39
9) Repetition along the Wall	42
X) Vote here: Is it Worth the Walk?	56

PART TWO: ROAMIN' — 63

Daily Distances, and O.S. Maps	64
An Introductory Day: West of the Wall	65
Wall Day One: To Bearsden (Premier Inn)	70
Wall Day Two: To Kirkintilloch (Smith's Hotel)	81
Wall Day Three: To Castlecary (Hotel)	89
How to Celebrate Victory	100
Wall Day Four: To Falkirk (Central Premier Inn)	104
Wall Day Five: To Beancross (Hotels)	113
Wall Day Six: To Carriden (House (B&B) & Fort)	118
The Garden Shed Syndrome	128
Extra Day: To Cramond	131
Accommodation	142
Trail by Train	146
Some Source Material	147

PREAMBLE & PRETEXT

It is easy to walk coast-to-coast across the narrow central belt of Scotland. It is not very far. It is not mountainous. Various authors have suggested routes: The cycle routes are good for cycling (but can have boring stretches for slow-moving walkers). The Forth and Clyde Canal plus Union Canal are often suggested (but the Union Canal follows contours which abhor straight lines). The John Muir Way from Helensburgh, via Loch Lomond, to Dunbar in East Lothian, wends its way across the land.

Thank goodness for the ancient Romans!

Emperor Antoninus Pius ordered the construction of a turf rampart and ditch which, with lots of forts in good look-out sites, form a great basis for our cross-country ramble. Books on the Antonine Wall tend to be written by archaeologists with an accurate eye for detail. Some books seem to hope the public will visit the better sites – often well cared for by Historic Scotland or the relevant local authority – but the usual assumption is that we shall come by car. The thing is this: Build a Wall of turf and/or clay and *don't expect it to be much in evidence after nearly 2,000 years.* As a result, you may be tempted to look *only* at the best bits, and it is hard to deny that cars are perfect vehicles for visiting the best bits of Wall and Fort. But, my guess is that **you** are built of sterner stuff!

This book is but one suggested compromise of a route for the walker, 'An Antonine Trail'. Having helped to lead walkers on long distance trails, I believe most folks enjoy pretty scenery, take an interest in fascinating sites or objects, appreciate variety, like a good story, look forward to the next coffee stop, and relish an evening's relaxation over an agreeable meal at a pleasant hostelry. To deliver these delights, we have scoured the literature and the countryside. Starting from a hypothetical attempt to 'Walk the Wall', we dodged the difficult bits and avoided built-up areas, so far as possible. We sought out pretty places and delightful diversions. We came across some convenient refreshment stops and – always believing that a continuous route is the way to proceed – we can recommend places to stop for the night. Some bits of our route go near to railway stations or bus routes so you can plan your exploration in stages. The one thing you have to do is PLAN AHEAD.

If you stroll slowly, you'll cover 10 miles (16 km) in 5 hours, including a coffee stop. For the nervous among you, the daily distances are gentle and are based purely on convenient overnight stops. Experienced walkers already know where they can usefully combine sections to create their own long walks. The accommodation list, at the back of the book, includes cumulative kilometres, so you can tailor-make your own lengths of daily walks. Just remember; you will want to linger at some spots to let your imagination dwell on the Roman soldiers who spent their careers looking after the edge of the Empire.

FALKIRK WHEEL BASIN

INTRODUCTION

I live in the village of Cramond in north Edinburgh where the River Almond discharges into the Firth of Forth. The Romans once lived here too, in their fort of Caer Almond, of which the modern name Cramond is a corruption. This fort was part of the Antonine Wall infrastructure.

Inspired by our Roman history, a Scout Show was presented at Cramond in 1964. This featured Julius Caesar's conquest of Britain* and, of course, a beautiful Pictish maiden's conquest of Caesar, in love. The show opened with Cramond students of history transported back in time to the Forum in Rome. The Romans' song, seemingly trite but, I suggest, with surprising historical accuracy regarding Roman campaigning went (to the tune of 'John Brown's Body'):

"*Senatus Populusque Romanus* is our flag.
We do not wish to conquer and we do not want to brag,
But when our soldiers go for you we've got you in the bag.
Veni. Vidi. Vici!

Chorus:
"Veni veni, vidi, vici
Veni veni, vidi, vici
Conquest seems so very easy
For mighty Julius C.

"Divide and Rule's the policy we Romans think is best.
Omnis Gallia, in three parts, *divisa est*.
We put a legion in; and leave to you the rest:
Veni. Vidi. Vici!"

Reproduced with the permission of the author/producer, Rev. Terence D C Large, M A.

*In 54 BC, Julius Caesar wrote *"Veni, vidi, vici"*. I came, I saw, I conquered. But *did he conquer us?* He got about as far as London, NOT Cramond; but he certainly started something.

AT THE END OF THE TRAIL: CRAMOND ROMAN FORT

CRAMOND KIRK IS BUILT ON THE FORT SITE

Why don't you take a leaf out of my book: or better still, take the whole book, and enjoy An Antonine Trail holiday? I have often been surprised at how folk are readily impressed and are often amazed when shown some of the good things left behind by the Romans.

In 2008, the Antonine Wall was incorporated into the World Heritage Site which already embraced Hadrian's Wall. Our Scottish Wall's proud new status had been helped of course by the fact that a lot of work, over several years, had brought it up to its present state. So what better time than *now* to take a look at it? Following all of the exact line of this Wall, on foot, is tricky for reasons we shall discover, but to adopt judicious diversions can be very well worth while. Trust me!

Can I be trusted? My wife and I run a walking group. Mostly we have one-day walks, but we have led groups on The West Highland Way, The Speyside Way, St.Cuthbert's Way, Offa's Dyke Path, Hadrian's Wall Path, The South Down's Way, The Saint Andrew's Way, The Cateran Trail, and now An Antonine Trail. Enjoy it: as *we* did!

This book is designed to conduct you across Scotland, coast-to-coast, taking a close look at *most* of the points of interest which we have inherited from the Romans. I think you will be delighted by what you find along the Trail. Notice that our title '*An* Antonine Trail' reflects the fact that we could have selected different ways from A to B. But I did say "Trust me"; so, I have, on your behalf, already walked various lines. I have selected this particular Trail route to offer you as much variety and pleasure as I can put together from the options available. I should advise you that we are going to miss out a section of hiking along the Wall-line into Duntocher (boring and partly a bus route). We shall also miss out bits of exposed Wall-base in Bearsden (housing estate) and New Kilpatrick Cemetery (busy road) though I do provide pictures of these; and we sometimes wander off line to preserve your sanity or your life or to enjoy canals or give you refreshment opportunities.

THE TRAIL BYPASSES THIS WALL BASE AT IAIN ROAD, BEARSDEN

AND THIS WALL BASE AT NEW KILPATRICK CEMETERY, BEARSDEN

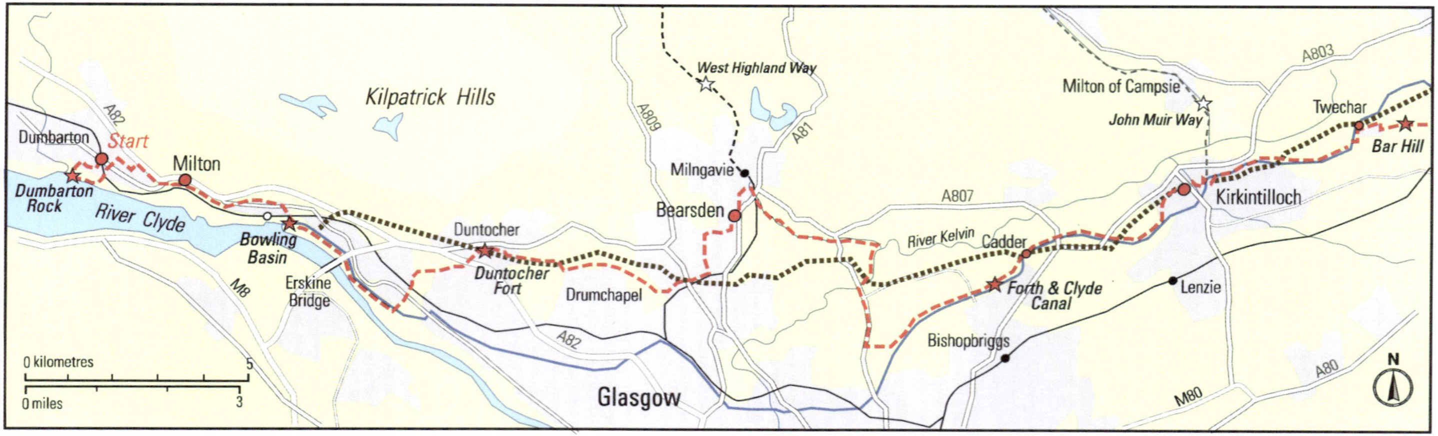
Kilpatrick Hills
Dumbarton
Start
Milton
A82
Dumbarton Rock
River Clyde
Bowling Basin
Erskine Bridge
M8
Duntocher
Duntocher Fort
Drumchapel
A82
Glasgow
West Highland Way
A809
A81
Milngavie
Bearsden
A807
River Kelvin
Cadder
Forth & Clyde Canal
Bishopbriggs
Lenzie
Milton of Campsie
John Muir Way
Kirkintilloch
A803
Twechar
Bar Hill
A80
M80
N
0 kilometres
5
0 miles
3

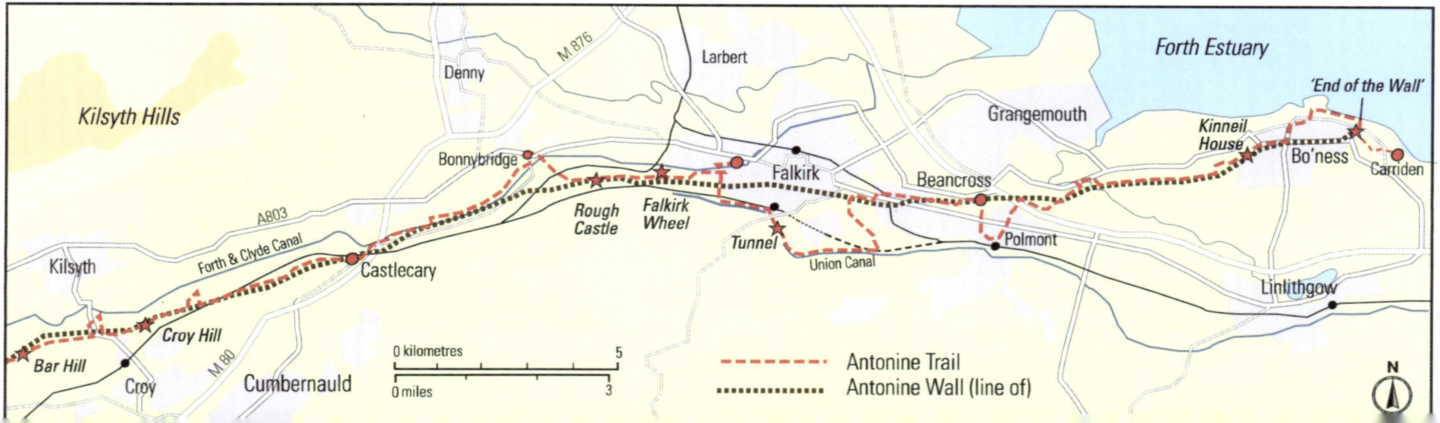
Kilsyth Hills
Kilsyth
Bar Hill
Croy
Croy Hill
M 80
Cumbernauld
A803
Forth & Clyde Canal
Castlecary
Denny
M 876
Bonnybridge
Rough Castle
Falkirk Wheel
Larbert
Falkirk
Tunnel
Union Canal
Grangemouth
Beancross
Polmont
Forth Estuary
Kinneil House
Bo'ness
'End of the Wall'
Carriden
Linlithgow
0 kilometres
5
0 miles
3
Antonine Trail
Antonine Wall (line of)
N

DISTANCES

The text, in PART TWO, fully explains all your options.

- Full Trail days have a Berger dot.
Wall Days Only have distances marked with an asterisk *

	Km	(miles)
• Introductory Day: To Milton	5	(3)
• Wall Day One: To Bearsden	20	(12)
{If starting at Bowling Station}	18.5*	(11)*
• Wall Day Two: To Kirkintilloch	16*	(10)*
• Wall Day Three: To Castlecary	16*	(10)*
• Wall Day Four: To Falkirk	14.5*	(9)*
• Wall Day Five: To Beancross	12*	(7½)*
{Combine Days 4 & 5; omit side visits}	20	(12)
• Wall Day Six: To Carriden	16	(10)
{To end of Wall in Harbour Road}	14*	(8½)*
• Extra Day: To Cramond	25	(15½)
{If cheating by hopping on the bus}	15.5	(9½)
• Full Trail distance	124.5	(77)
Wall Days Only distance	91*	(56)*

PART ONE

PART ONE

ROMAN

Long distance walkers are often in a hurry. They clearly *like* the walking but they are driven to get it over and done with!

In Part One, I suppose I want to soften you up a bit to try to make you *want* to slow down in order to look at some of what remains of this Roman frontier in Scotland. If one takes a group of malt whisky drinkers along the Speyside Way – although the very word 'Speyside' will set their nostrils twitching – they will be in such a hurry to complete each day's walk on time that they will not wish to spend, or waste time visiting distilleries! I hope that *you* – sober history lovers – will drink in the Roman delights along our Antonine Trail, making plenty of time available to fulfil your task.

So, we start with some background. I have already mentioned Julius Caesar who never came to Scotland but certainly landed in Britain. He may have thought of it as 'Alba': it is the feminine ending for the Latin adjective for chalky white or egg white (whence albumen), a perfect description of part of the south coast.

Caesar conquered Gaul and he said he conquered Britain. One could argue that his career led to the entire system of Roman Emperors and, indeed, the Empire. Julius was not himself an Emperor; his adopted Augustus became the next Caesar and was the first Emperor. Our language comes from Latin; our Rule of Law from Rome. Civilisation is Italian; it implies forming cities (Latin *civis* = citizen).

My first two sections of Part One offer the 'softening' process, I mentioned. My third section introduces frontiers; with my fourth introducing my account of the effect of Roman Rewards. Three sections discuss The Antonine Wall and later happenings. Another section relates the West-to-East Wall with the West-to-East Canal.

We conclude Part One with a 'repetitive essay' and we vote on doing the walking Trail.

1) VENI VIDI VICI

These three neat little words which we met in the Introduction are how Julius Caesar summed up his visits to Britain in 55 and 54 BC: "I came; I saw; I conquered". English pilfered Latin words, wholesale. Thus: from *veni* <u>adventure</u>, from *vidi* <u>vision</u>, and from *vici* <u>victory</u>.

Now, Julius Caesar didn't exactly find Britain the proverbial walkover (as *we* shall!). Despite planning; when he arrived in 55 BC with nearly a hundred ships, his cavalry's ships were delayed; so Caesar's two infantry legions, which had landed, were forced to retreat. The next year, 54 BC, Caesar narrowed the odds: his fleet was several hundreds of boats and he'd got *four* legions and nearly two thousand horsemen, and horses. This time he conquered beyond London and got rewarded back in Rome. Indeed, the title 'Caesar' was so prestigious it was used in Germany as 'Kaiser' and in Russia as 'Czar' (5/10 for spelling), or Tsar (3/10).

We may find it helpful to bear in mind how well-organised the Romans were. They liked to have structure, organisation, laws, systems, method, and communications. A network of roads, linking cities and forts, set the spatial framework – of which the Antonine Wall forms a part. Their temporal framework utilised days, weeks, and months – the Calendar. Our next section looks at the Roman calendar – *our* Calendar.

2) ITS A DATE, AND OTHER NUMBERS

Before Julius Caesar was murdered, ten years after leaving Britain, he sorted the calendar – before his successor, his adopted Augustus Caesar – messed it up. *Very* ancient Romans seem to have reckoned on a year of ten months, starting in March, with a sort of dead period over winter. Each year, someone clever had to declare the new crop-planting season and a new beginning. The names of the seventh to tenth months were September, October, November, December; based on the Roman numbers 7 = *septem*, 8 = *octo*, 9 = *novem*, 10 = *decem*. First, Caesar figured – well, he employed a man – that the year should have 365 days, with 366 in leap years. He started in March to which he assigned 31 days, April got 30 days. In fact, the year ran with, alternately, months of 31, 30, 31, 30 . . . days right through. On a leap year, the *last* month of the year, *February*, got an extra day; or, rather, it was one day short if it was *not* a leap year. Focus your eye on the number of days in each month.

So, a leap year went:-
MAR=31 APR=30 MAY=31 JUN=30 JUL=31 AUG=30 SEP=31 OCT=30 NOV=31 DEC=30 JAN=31 FEB=30 (29, if *not* a leap year)

How about that for neat and tidy? By the way, the month of August didn't yet bear that name. Can you guess how Augustus messed up the neat system that Julius had created?

We may note that Julius chose a nice summer month *with 31 days* and named it after himself, JULIUS (July). It happened to be the fifth month of the year and *had* been called *Quintilis* (Latin 5 = *quinque*). Obviously, Augustus had to be upsides with his predecessor Julius. So Augustus named the very next summer month, the sixth month, after *himself,* AUGUSTUS (August). It had been called *Sextilis* (Latin 6 = *sex*) AND he decreed that it must *also* have 31 days because he was very important, too! Then, he restarted the alternating lengths of months with September having only 30 days. By this time, the year was reckoned to start with January which, in view of this importance, had to keep its 31 days. February was, nevertheless, still reckoned as the tag-end month – which kindly supplied the extra day for August. For comparison with the original Julian calendar, I shall keep March up front. Again, focus on the numbers.

Now, our leap year goes:-
MAR=31 APR=30 MAY=31 JUN=30 JUL=31 AUG=31 SEP=30 OCT=31 NOV=30 DEC=31 JAN=31 FEB=29 (28, if not a leap year)

How about that for a total mess? No one has ever been strong enough to put it all back. Now we have to make up silly rhymes that go:

"Thirty days hath September,
April, June, and November.
February has twenty eight days clear;
And twenty nine in each leap year."

I bet that caused a pain for the first person writing the software for a digital calendar. Amazingly, we in Scotland are still so fixated on the *old* start of the year in March, that, as all parents in Scotland know, a child's birth after a date in March determines which year they start school. If you're born in January or February, you start school a year earlier.

All I have to say about the 'Other Numbers' of this section's heading is: Have you ever tried to multiply XXVII by XIII without resorting to our convenient Arabic numerals: 27 times 13 = ?

But now we shall deal with the number VII in the next section.

First, we should mention a different "Callendar". The Antonine Trail and Wall make their way past "Callendar House" in Wall Day Five – see Part Two.

CALLENDAR HOUSE FROM THE TRAIL ALONG THE WALL

THE ANTONINE DITCH AS IT PASSES CALLENDAR HOUSE, FALKIRK

3) SEVEN IS A BIG NUMBER

We have noted that Julius Caesar declared "Vici" (I conquered). And he got his Reward from Rome for this. But he left a lot of work still to be done.

Even after four centuries, Romans had failed to conquer all of Britannia. Because of this, they always had to keep a weather eye on what the barbarians further north were up to. I've asked various folk how many frontiers the Romans set up across Britain. I am thinking from my Scottish perspective, here – so am excluding, for instance, Offa's Dyke which runs down the English border with Wales, and which some consider to have been engineered by the Romans a few hundred years before King Offa of Mercia was born. The usual answer to my question is "one" or "two", referring to Hadrian's Wall and/or the Antonine Wall.

Now here's a thing! They always seem to place the definite article before 'Antonine': "The Antonine Wall". I cannot recall seeing "Antonine's Wall" in print. Furthermore, I am certain I have never read "The Hadrian Wall"; it's always "Hadrian's Wall". Have archaeologists adopted a convention to demonstrate how meticulously exact and careful they all are? Or does "Hadrian's Wall" reflect the fact that Emperor Hadrian arrived in person to determine the Wall's position and make sure work started? He was certainly the ultimate hands-on meddler, and not so popular because of it. And does "The Antonine Wall" reflect the fact that Emperor Antoninus Pius ordered that *that* Wall be built *without* coming in person. Indeed, *he* was the supreme delegator: he never left Italy.

So, how many frontiers can we count? Here is a list of Roman frontiers in north Britain, hopefully in the order of building or occupation. You can also refer to the Roman Frontiers Map.

Roman Frontiers in North Britain

map shows only *six* frontiers. The Agricolan Forts – item (2) overleaf – tend to lie
[und]er the Antonine Wall and cannot be shown separately at this scale.

(1) AD 73?   A line of signalling towers along a track/road stretching from Doune to Perth (Bertha), including three or four forts. This has been called the Gask Frontier and is quite possibly the earliest 'fortified' frontier in the Roman Empire.

(2) AD 81.   A line of sporadic forts, possibly built by Agricola – of whom more later – more or less close to the line of the later Antonine Wall, so not shown separately on our map.

(3) AD 84.   A line of eight or nine forts, seemingly plugging the mouths of Highland glens. Let's call this the Highland Frontier.

(4) AD 90?   An array of about half a dozen forts stretching from Dumfriesshire northwest to Newstead (Melrose, or Trimontium to the Romans) which seems to have been held as an area of defence. Let's refer to it as the Border Outpost.

(5) AD 105.   A line of eight or nine forts along the Stanegate road from Carlisle to Corbridge: The Stanegate Frontier.

(6) AD 122.   Hadrian's Wall: A 120 km stone wall from Bowness-on-Solway to Wallsend, with forts, milecastles, turrets, and a western extension of forts without any wall.

(7) AD 142.   The Antonine Wall: A 60 km turf wall from Old Kilpatrick to Bo'ness, with primary and secondary forts.

This is much simplified. It *has to be* for my memory to cope. Let me exemplify the complications: When the Antonine Wall was built in 142, Hadrian's Wall was abandoned, as if for ever. But the Romans moved back to Hadrian's Wall and abandoned the Antonine Wall. Seven may be a big number, but 7 + 1 = 8 is bigger!

And look at the time scale. Romans occupied these shores for about half a millennium, but in just over seventy years they moved frontiers up and down the land like a yo-yo.

Can we find some motivation for the making of these boundary changes?

4) REWARDS FROM ROME

Even fastidious archaeologists are prone to follow fads.
   Once upon a time, we all believed that Roman frontiers were built for defence. One can imagine Roman soldiers, with their swords at the ready on top of their wall, prepared to cut down any barbarian with the temerity to try and scale the defence. But the Romans – usually – had considerable reserves of manpower and could head north beyond their own frontier to subdue misbehaving tribes whenever they chose. So the modern picture is of a controlled territory, not only south of the frontier, but extending north, too. Thus, our frontier is a line of customs posts where the peasantry (I shouldn't wish to be offensive, but they were in fact plebeians) – where the peasantry would have to pay dues on the movement of goods or livestock, in either direction.
   The whole point of the Roman army was that it survived by moving forward; scooping up resources of the conquered to fuel the Roman economy; then repeating the process. Static frontiers meant taxing people who *did* require to move for trade, to add to revenues gleaned from an otherwise static population. And revenues were really important. Did you know: if you were a Roman citizen, living in Rome, you were provided with *free food*! Our Chancellor of the Exchequer falls a tad short of this, does he not?
   Sorry, everyone, but I have a *third* model of frontier function. The model came to me when I had been trying to explain British frontier variations – the 'yo-yo' – to a group of Cramond walkers shivering near Croy Hill. They found the story amusing. Was there any engine which drove the Roman frontier up and down the land almost literally like a yo-yo, and over the space of only seventy years or so? Yes, I think so: Rewards from Rome. Are you sitting comfortably?

Emperor Claudius ordered a fresh invasion, in 43 AD, some 97 years after Julius Caesar's. His commander was a chap called Vespasian, a future emperor. (Yes, he got *his* Reward.) The focus of attack was Colchester, in Essex; the town being then called

Camulodonum and the capital of the kingdom of Cunobelinus, the very same person whom William Shakespeare called Cymbeline. Shakespeare may have been a great playwright but his spelling could be rickety – even of his *own* name. ('Shakspere' is but one of three variants.) Emperor Claudius seems to have been a bit of a play-actor, too. He had some great stage management. Although he was in Britain just over a fortnight, he appeared in person with his secret weapon: elephants! Then, after he had won; no fewer than *eleven* British kings offered obeisance, including one from Orkney! How on earth did he stage-manage *that*? Well, Claudius's Empire quite obviously extended to the edge of the world. Rewards indeed in his triumphal procession next year in Rome.

When Vespasian became emperor he appointed a new governor of Britain, Cerialis, who arrived in AD 71. He may have been accompanied by Gnaeus Julius Agricola. Either Cerialis or Agricola set up the Gask Frontier (see previous section) in Scotland. If it was in 73 AD, my money is on Cerialis who, the same year returned to Rome (Reward?) to be replaced by governor Frontinus. Agricola went on to become a provincial governor in Gaul; but returned to Britain in the late 70s.

Agricola was a character. Apart from being well in with Vespasian he allowed his daughter to marry one, Tacitus, the historian. So we have a good record of Agricola – good for Agricola, good for Rewards from Rome, and good for Tacitus.

Well, Vespasian died in AD 79 and was, eventually, succeeded by Domitian who seems to have authorised Agricola's sweep up the north of England and the east of Scotland. Here's what Tacitus has told us about Agricola. He organised parallel advances northwards: from Carlisle up the route of the modern M74 and from Corbridge up the modern A68 route. They were at the River Tay in AD 79. About AD 81, Agricola had built a line of forts (previous section) on a similar sort of line to the future Antonine Wall.

Agricola set up a line of marching camps up the east of Scotland but seems to have supplied his forces by sea. In AD 83, he won a great victory over the Caledonians, who were led by Calgacus; at a place Tacitus called Mons Graupius. Although the actual battle site has never been identified (yet), many Scots would detect a remarkable similarity between our well kent 'Grampian Mountains' and Tacitus's 'Mons Graupius'. You are probably already saying:

"Aha! Tacitus must have heard it incorrectly or wrote it down wrongly; he must have meant 'Mons Gra<u>m</u>pius'." Surprise, surprise; it turns out that an early editor of Tacitus's *Agricola* made the error by writing 'Grampian'. Tacitus had been right all the time. *We* are the ones who should have been talking about 'The Gra<u>u</u>pian Mountains', for our name for the range has been derived from Tacitus! I find the details of this Roman victory in battle endearing and amusing and typically Roman. Calgacus had 30,000 men. The Romans had 8,000 infantry and 3,000 cavalry. The *foreign* auxiliary forces fronted the Roman attack. Agricola kept his actual *Roman* legionaries safely in reserve. When the cavalry started circling the Highlanders, the remaining brave Caledonians melted off into the hills. At the end of the day: Caledonians lying dead numbered 10,000; the Roman army suffered 360 deaths. Time for more Rewards from Rome?

Domitian, the Roman Emperor as you will recall; had a large triumphal arch built where Claudius had first started out with his elephants in AD 43. It was clad in marble and had golden statues and a footing is still visible.

COLCHESTER'S 'HOLE IN THE WALL' PUB IS BUILT ON TOP OF THE BLOCKED-UP LOCATION OF DOMITIAN'S TRIUMPHAL ARCH

**SITE OF NORTH CARRIAGEWAY ARCH IS UNDER THE PUB TERRACE
THE ORIGINAL FOOTING IS ABOVE THE WEEDS ON THE RIGHT**

So that was Britain conquered, eh? Hmmm, *third time*, by my reckoning. Let's be clear, these Roman Rewards were for Domitian, himself. What about our hero, Agricola? He was ordered to Rome to arrive at the palace *after dark* where Domitian surreptitiously kissed him, then sent him back out into the night!

With the withdrawal from Britain of both Agricola and Tacitus, *we* were left in the dark, too. We stopped getting the written reports. We know the Romans' plan was to settle in Scotland. They built the Highland Frontier forts mentioned in the previous section, no doubt with the intention of future advances. This included the vast Inchtutil Legionary fort, started in 84 AD. But it was never finished; two years later they dismantled buildings and went off on some other errand. Tacitus did report that Britain had been conquered but then set free!

Now we turn to Emperor Trajan. His Reward from Rome can still be seen *in* Rome: Trajan's column (even if the top bit did fall off – about a quarter of it, since you ask. Don't panic; it was put back on.) Trajan reigned from 98 to 117 AD. There's not much evidence of his being interested in Britain. In fact, he swiped a legion for use elsewhere.

TRAJAN'S COLUMN (centre) TRAJAN'S FORUM, ROME

By around the turn of the century we find evidence of the Stanegate. It means 'stone-paved road', and it ran from Carlisle to Corbridge along east-west valleys. One famous fort on it was Vindolanda, modern name Chesterholm, where we've all heard about the finds of actual Roman handwritten letters: "I'm sending socks and underpants." That sort of thing. Trajan's endeavours actually left this fort empty for a month until reinforcements arrived. Well, you know the saying: "When the cat's away the mice will play." So the natives had a field day, destroying forts down Dere Street (the A68 line) and setting Corbridge on fire. Nevertheless, refurbishment of the Stanegate forts seems to have been carried out. Trajan's death in AD 117 was another excuse for trouble in Britain.

The new Emperor Hadrian was a truly dynamic man, a great traveller, a hands-on-operator, and a renowned homosexual. He arrived in Britain in person in AD 122, probably sailing into the River Tyne (Newcastle) with his wife – yes wife – Sabina and, probably, his new governor, Platorius Nepos. Hadrian was a consolidator. He had been with Trajan when Persia was conquered. (A digression now; but strictly to the point! You may have heard that film directors, when marshalling crowds of extras who are to be filmed chattering to one another, sometimes instruct these cast extras to mutter continually the word 'rhubarb', thus: "Rhubarb, rhubarb, rhubarb, rhubarb . . ." You may notice the frequent repetition of the syllable "barb". Now, when Trajan was in Persia, the Roman troops rather agreed with the Greek view that Persians' chattering sounded like: "Barb, barb, barb, barb . . ." So, dear reader, the Persians became the first 'bar<u>b</u>arians'.) But Hadrian let these bar-bar-barians free again. He later built a fence in Germany from the Danube to the Rhine. Britain got the Wall. Hadrian seems to have specified *that* the Wall should be built, and *where*, and *how*. Its situation was north of the old Stanegate, on a ridge where there may have been watchtowers like the ones on the Gask Frontier, but now of course, obliterated by the new Wall. If you want to study this frontier, you could do worse than walking Hadrian's Wall Path. Warning: that National Trail is written from east to west. Our sensible walking group started from the west from Bowness-on-Solway and walked to the east at Wallsend. On a couple of days with the prevailing wind and rain on our backs we met National Trail followers coming towards us with driving rain in their faces.

Hadrian nominated his successors: Antoninus Pius, a rather unwilling Emperor, a wealthy estate owner in his early fifties; to be followed by Marcus Aurelius who was, at first, far too young. Hadrian died in 138 AD. He had not been popular. His retirement complex in a magnificent and vast estate at Tivoli outside Rome was regarded as extravagant and quite over-the-top. I am not aware of Hadrian's winning any Reward from Rome other, of course, than the monument which he created: his astonishing Wall which, I suppose, offers Rewards galore.

Even though Antonine appointed a new governor of Britain, Lollius Urbicus, the Empire had taken its eye off the ball and there seems to have been some sort of revolt. 139 AD saw Urbicus rebuilding at Corbridge and in 142 a Roman military victory was commemorated on new coins. Antonine was smart. He was such a good delegator that – unlike Hadrian – he never left Italy till his death in 161. Antonine did the popular thing. Romans were supposed to *advance* not *retrench*. Also, he knew the Romans' allies north of Hadrian's Wall were the Votadini who had power bases at Yeavering Bell in the Cheviot Hills; and at Traprain Law and, I suppose, on the Rock where Edinburgh Castle sits – both south of the Firth of Forth. They, poor things, had been shut out of Empire by Hadrian's Wall. So, a mere twenty years after Hadrian's Wall started building, Antonine – or his man, Lollius Urbicus – was building a *new wall* from the Clyde to the Forth. Thus, the Roman Empire had advanced *and* the Votadini were included. One neat embellishment was refurbishing forts on the old Gask Frontier, so that the Venicones, friendly Roman-day Fifers, were also included. So: Rewards from Rome for Antonine then, by public acclaim. Also, he did erect a temple to his wife Faustina. You can still see it in the Forum in Rome, though in later years it was dedicated also to Antoninus. It is probably the most complete building of the ancient Forum.

There you have it! You shift the frontier up or down and you collect your Rewards from Rome. To me, the system seems to have worked well.

TEMPLE OF ANTONINUS AND FAUSTINA, THE FORUM, ROME

5) CHRONOLOGY WAS THE PROBLEM

Before we discuss the Antonine Wall, we should say a word about words: The similarity between Latin *vallum* and English 'wall' is obvious, especially as *v* in Latin was pronounced "w" so the Latin word sounded like "wallum". In fact *vallum* was originally a pallisaded wall; the word having come from *vallus* a 'stake'. First, we need to know a little about the earlier Hadrian's Wall, (built twenty years before the Antonine Wall). It was of stone and it, too, had a Ditch to its north: but it also had a demarcation line running parallel to the south and often separated from the Wall itself by hundreds of metres; so that a zone of military control was created. This line of control comprised a flat-bottomed ditch with a mound on each side: Mound-Ditch-Mound, where the main feature is the Ditch. (Our Antonine Wall managed fine without this military control zone).

What do we call this demarcation Ditch? Er, *"The Vallum"*! I may be digging a hole for myself here, if not, a ditch. So, who is responsible for this name?

Our eighth century historian who endeavoured to practise tenacious exactness, the Venerable Bede of Jarrow, is our man. He was unaware of our – relatively modern – attribution of Walls to Hadrian and Antonine. Bede thought this *"Vallum"*, or southern demarcation feature, was *the sum total of the FIRST Roman Wall* and he thought Severus built it. He called it *"The Vallum"*: The Wall. And so do we! To save you all from attending a master-class in Bede's version of history, suffice it to say that Bede seems to have thought that the SECOND LAST Wall to be built was our own Antonine Wall, but he didn't know the man responsible. And – again without attribution – he thought the actual stone (Hadrian's) Wall running parallel to, and north of, his *"Vallum"*, was a *THIRD* Wall! Bede's conclusions all seem reasonable to me; apart from the fact that they were all wrong!

To complete our confusion, the Romans called a ditch *fossa* (from which 'fossicking' or digging-around derives). 'Valley' comes from Latin *vallis* – completely different!

6) ABOUT THE ANTONINE WALL

Work started in 142 AD with, you will recall, Lollius Urbicus in charge. This would have been some three centuries earlier than our friend the Venerable Bede had been led to believe. Chronology is so much easier when you know the answers.

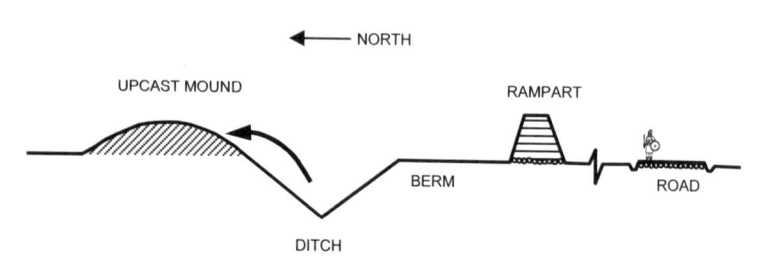

```
                    ◄──── NORTH
    UPCAST MOUND                    RAMPART
      ╱╲                              ╱╲
     ╱░░╲                            ╱░░╲           👤
  ──╱░░░░╲──────╲      ╱────────────░░░░░────╲ ╱───────────
              ╲    ╱            BERM              ROAD
               ╲  ╱
                ╲╱
               DITCH
```

In walking the first 'Wall Day' you won't see *any* Wall, unless from Castle Hill. Let's start with what we think the Romans built. They built a turf wall. Someone has come across a Roman manual specifying turf dimensions: pieces of turf that I should have difficulty lifting. They were desirably, apparently, 150mm or 6 inches thick. Archaeologists have identified some 20 layers of turf in the Wall. It was once thought that 20 layers of turf at 150mm (or 6 inches) thick, make a wall 3m (or 10 feet) tall. Turf bricks get squashed, whether or not they are really 150mm at the start. The arithmetic may have 'stacked up', to coin a phrase. But the natural squashing effect reduces the height to 2 or 2.5m (6 to 8 feet).

Most of the Wall east from Falkirk was built from clay with turf sides. No one knows why. The Wall got narrower towards the top. Some unknowns: Could you walk along the top? Was there a palisade on top? Was it important not easily to see over it? In front, north, of the Wall was a berm – usually about 6m wide. In front of that the Ditch was dug, generally some 6 to 10 metres wide and about 4m deep. Without our modern machinery, that is a *serious* piece of excavation. Material from the Ditch was cast out to the north, effectively deepening the Ditch. Behind the Wall, to the south, and varying distances from it (20 to 40m) ran the Military Way, a road some 5m wide surfaced with stones and gravel and furnished with drainage ditches. The road may have been constructed first. A likely scenario (though no one knows) is that the Antonine Wall took three or four years to build, with additional forts (see next paragraph) being added from year two or year three. Some work was being carried out at least as late as 155 AD, some 13 years after the commencement of works.

The Wall was provided with forts. Some forts which had been built earlier were connected with the Wall. In the initial design, forts were built very approximately eight miles apart with fortlets at (presumed) mile intervals. Some forts were built before the Wall arrived. E.g. Old Kilpatrick. At Balmuildy and at Mumrills, wing-walls projected to attach to the forthcoming Wall. But here's the thing: Balmuildy had a *stone* rampart around it (so had Castlecary); all the other forts have turf ramparts. Perhaps the original intention was to build another stone Wall, like Hadrian's, but the turf scheme won. Another design-change added forts, reducing the average spacing to rather over two miles. That's a lot more forts! Plan A had 7 or 8 forts and plan B 17. Bar Hill fort is rather out of position and a bit close to Croy Hill fort: it, also, does not connect with the Wall.

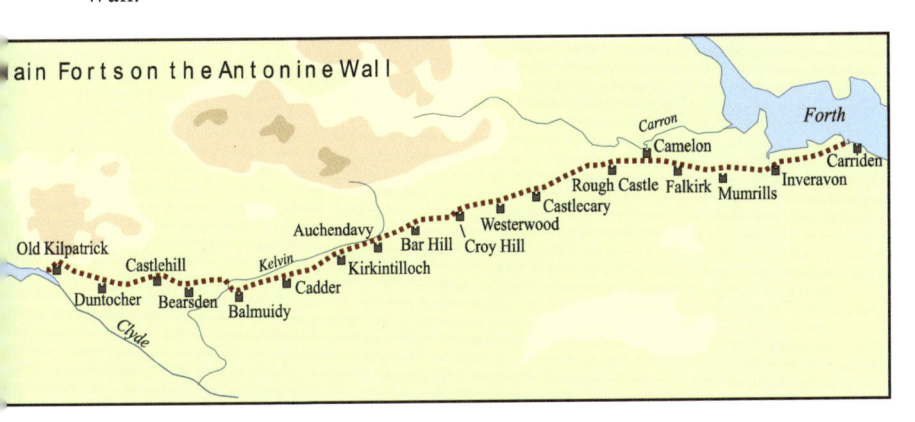

Main Forts on the Antonine Wall

With the new Wall, from Old Kilpatrick to Bo'ness, only half the length of Hadrian's, they could afford almost double the concentration of manpower per kilometre: 6 or 7 thousand men along 60 km, compared with 8 thousand along 120 km. Most Antonine forts got annexes to house more men, or horses, or civilian servicing personnel. The Antonine Wall seems to have been a more user-friendly design than Hadrian's: it was a better design. The Wall was effectively 'stretched' at each end with outlier forts: in the west, south of the Clyde on an eminence a mile or so west of Bishopton, and on Lurg Moor 250 metres above sea level on the hills south of Greenock; and in the east, at Cramond on the River Almond and at Inveresk on the River Esk, both rivers being tributaries of the River Forth. As we have seen, the friendly Votadini – excluded by Hadrian – were now included in the empire. Lollius Urbicus seems to have added another 'welcoming' touch. He titivated the original Gask Frontier, occupying the forts at Ardoch, Strageath, and Cargill north-west of Perth. So the friendly Venicones in Fife could feel included, too.

I can tell you the Roman name of only *one* fort on the Antonine Wall (although for Hadrian's Wall *all* the Roman names have been identified). A list of Roman names does exist for ten towns across the narrow neck of Britain from Forth to Clyde: unfortunately, there were seventeen forts. Within my lifetime, an inscription *Velunia* was found at Carriden Fort at the east end of the Antonine Wall. This also happens to be the first Roman name on the list of ten towns. Carriden was *Velunia* to the Romans. So, more work must be done.

7) WHAT HAPPENED NEXT?

With the Antonine Wall fully functioning, the mighty stone Hadrian's Wall seems to have been abandoned. Since it was then no longer a barrier/custom's frontier – they removed milecastle gates and so forth. But they *did* hold onto Carlisle, Vindolanda, and Corbridge, along the Stanegate. A bit like pre-Hadrian times, then?

Presently, a funny thing happened. We may assume Roman forces were now over-stretched, and they were expensive. So, from around 158 AD, preparations were being made on the old Hadrian's Wall to receive troops. Yes, they were rebuilding/refurbishing. Emperor Antoninus Pius had ordered a return to Hadrian's Wall. Antonine Wall forts were burned or rendered unusable. The actual Ditch and Wall were simply abandoned. Except: Cramond Fort, Camelon Fort (north from the gate at Watling Lodge Fortlet), and Newstead by Trimontium on Dere Street (Melrose) seem to have remained occupied. In 161, Antonine died. He was succeeded by Marcus Aurelius, whom Hadrian had nominated to follow Antonine, and who was now sufficiently mature. In AD 180, *his* son Commodus Antonius succeeded. He was as daft as a brush and was assassinated in 192. In 197, after a battle over succession, Septimius Severus became Emperor.

We know Septimius Severus was African; he was born in the Roman city of Leptis Magna on the coast of what is modern Libya; we know he was 51; and we know he had gout. Right away (197 AD) he literally bought time, i.e. peace, in Britain by getting his new Governor, Virius Lupus, to bribe the Maeatae and Caledonii. (The Maeatae seem to have been in the area of the Gask Frontier, with the Caledonii further north-west.)

Ten years later, in 207 AD, there seems to have been really serious trouble and the, now, new Governor, Alfenus Senecio, called for Help with a capital 'H'. After great preparation, Severus arrived in person in 208 AD with his sleeves rolled up. He brought the family: wife Julia and sons Caracalla and Geta. He also had a huge army and a huge fleet. His base was York but he built twenty three new granaries at South Shields Fort, south of the River Tyne but east of Newcastle, which could supply 40,000 men for three months. So, he meant business! He refurbished Corbridge on the Dere Street (A68) line and, as his army moved northwards up Dere Street, they built marching camps, each over 150 acres. It was said that as each new camp was being set up by the van-guard of the marching line, the rear-guard was still leaving the previous camp. The fleet came up in parallel bringing supplies. Cramond Fort was refurbished and was visited by Septimius Severus. The vast army moved north from the River Forth, presumably via Camelon and, to cut a long story short, probably reached the Moray Firth. There seem to have been skirmishes but there was no repeat of the big battle of Agricola's Mons Graupius. They seem to have advanced leisurely, flattening routes through trees and building bridges; possibly even floating one, using boats tethered across the River Tay at Carpow. They must have exacted tribute: land in Strathmore was taken over by Rome, and Scottish conscripts were in Germany many years later.

In 210 AD, victory was celebrated. Severus, Caracalla and Geta each got the title 'Britannicus'. Severus died in York in 211. When Caracalla took his Dad's ashes and the remainder of the family home to Rome, two Scottish forts were still in business: Cramond, south of the Forth, and Carpow, south of the Tay. Moving forwards nearly 100 years, it has been said that at both these forts there is evidence of a Roman advance north by 306 AD by Emperor Constantius Chlorus, accompanied by his son, Constantine (the Great). The grandson, Chlorus, came to Britain in 342/3 and seems to have been at Hadrian's Wall.

By 407, the empire was in disarray but in 410 AD, efficient Roman civil servants wrote letters to British cities to suggest they defend themselves. And that was that.

8) IF THE ROMANS HAD HAD A FORTH AND CLYDE CANAL

You know how it is: unless you were an ancient Roman, large construction projects tended to be discussed *ad nauseam* for years or decades before things started to move forward. Our Roman conquerors may have dug a big ditch from the Forth to the Clyde but they never thought of filling it with water and sailing along it. That thought had to wait till King Charles II's reign. Mind you, if the Romans had only thought to dig a *level* ditch, instead of one going up hill and down dale, it was otherwise of sufficient cross-section to fill with water and float one's boat!

It wasn't until the mid 18th century that the idea for a canal started to move forward. John Smeaton, the civil engineer, was asked to draw up a proposal for a 'wide' (as opposed to 'narrow') canal to join the Forth with the Clyde – or was it to join the Clyde with the Forth? The point I am aiming at here is that the notion had the unexpected achievement of stirring up Edinburgh/Glasgow rivalry. To appreciate the feelings of the time, you have to realise that the River Clyde was too shallow to be navigable by sizeable vessels further up than the vicinity of Bowling/Erskine/Old Kilpatrick. In ancient times you could *ford* the river here at low tide. This is why The Antonine Wall had to start here; and is also the reason why the canal had to start here, too. It is true that smaller vessels *could* get up to Glasgow. (Big ships had to wait for deeper and deeper dredging, culminating with the dredging required for the launching of the Queen Mary in the 1930s). Our Glasgow traders worried that the WIDE canal proposal might well come from the Forth to the Clyde but might bypass Glasgow. This would give Edinburgh traders access to both east and west but would hem Glasgow traders into the west – and the Clyde – with no exit to the east. These thrifty Glaswegians came up with a cunning cut-price plan. Why not build an economical NARROW canal; but running from central Glasgow – *not the Clyde* – to the Forth via the River Carron? Now, Glasgow could trade east via canal, or west by the Clyde. Edinburgh would be penned in the east. Smart idea, eh?

Sense prevailed. What they built was the originally intended 'wide' canal, from the Clyde at Bowling to the Forth at Grangemouth, but with a branch going into central Glasgow. Now traders from either city could sail east or west. Job done. Funnily enough, the enabling Act of Parliament, of 1768, included provision for an eastern branch continuing to Bo'ness – just like the Antonine Wall! But that branch was never built. It took twenty two years to complete the canal although, for a third of that time nothing happened – nae money! I shouldn't wish to start religious division, but you will recall Bonnie Prince Charlie's attempted coup in 1745. When the rebellion was crushed, some estates were impounded. The money for the canal came from selling forfeited estates. The wide Forth and Clyde Canal was completed in 1790. In 1822, the narrow Union Canal united central Edinburgh with the Forth and Clyde Canal above the latter's Lock 16 at Port Downie, a substantial basin – now infilled.

FORTH AND CLYDE CANAL PASSES CADDER FORT SITE

A new British Waterways Board took over both canals in 1962, but at the very start of 1963 an act of parliament extinguished all rights of navigation. Was there some kind of conspiracy? You bet there was. That very same year, 1963, the construction of the (then) A80 dual carriageway closed the canal entirely – except for the important flow of water – at Castlecary. A scary place, Castlecary; this breach was but yards from the spot where the railway had sliced through the middle of the Roman fort site.

THE A 80 (NOW M 80) WAS RAISED TO CLEAR BOATS

To cut a long story short, volunteers and tub-thumpers along the canal persuaded the powers-that-be to restore the Forth and Clyde and Union Canals – after further dereliction and physical obstructions – as a 'millennium project'. Whence came the amazing, crowd-pulling, civil engineering attraction, the Falkirk Wheel, the modern way of overcoming the difference in levels of, and restoring the physical link between, these two canals. I guess we were lucky that 1990 was the wide canal's 200th anniversary, nicely timed to give a ten year's run-up to a year 2000 boat-launching ceremony, just a wee bit ahead of the completion of the restoration works. This time, funding came from lots of good folks who had purchased lottery tickets. Our stroll across Scotland makes use of a few sections of both canals and passes the Falkirk Wheel. I trust this toe-dipping exercise will help launch you on your way.

9) REPETITION ALONG THE WALL

In preparing this book, I was struck by the persistent continuity of the Wall and Ditch – especially the Ditch because it has endured better. As you walk the Wall, day by day, you can hardly fail to be impressed by the sheer effort put into its construction by the Roman legionaries.

I was also struck by certain repetitive features. These included the Forts, certainly; but in this section we shall consider three other repetitive features:

> **The word *Caere***
> **Distance slabs**
> **Ordinary building stones and their recycling**

The Word *Caere*
In Italy, 50km north-west of Rome, we find modern Cerveteri. At this place, and pre-dating the founding of Rome (753 BC), stood the powerful Etruscan fortified town of *CAERE*. The inhabitants of Caere seem to have been pre-occupied with rituals about religion and prophecy. This gave rise to a Latin word *caeremonium* from which we derive our English word 'ceremony'.

The English and, indeed, Welsh make liberal use of the word *Caere*, usually as a prefix and denoting a castle or fortification: Caernarfon and Caerphilly being prime examples in Wales, where one may readily come across another dozen.

In Roman times on the Antonine Wall, some local people – like the Votadini – spoke a form of Welsh and, presumably as a result of that, the word *Caere* is evident at some Fort sites on the Wall. Before we offer up our prospective list of these, we should remember that the Romans had, not surprisingly, their own names for their own Forts, none of which contained the word *Caere*. We should conclude, therefore, that names containing *Caere* must have been generated and attached to some sites in post-Roman times.

Here is the prospective list of *Caere* fort sites:

KIRKINTILLOCH	The first syllable is corrupted from 'Caer'; it has nothing to do with Church!
CROY HILL	All I can say is, the CR and Y look a bit suspicious to me.
CASTLECARY	The 'cary' is *caere*, tautologically joined to 'Castle'. The medieval tower house of Castle Cary is written as two words – but equally tautologically.
CARRIDEN	The first two syllables, 'Carri' are really *Caere*.
CRAMOND	The CR is again *Caere*.

Distance Slabs

The stone slabs, on which our Wall-builders proudly proclaimed the length *they* had built, are now collected in museums in Glasgow and Edinburgh, so will not be found on our Trail. However, a modern laser-cut facsimile of the eastmost slab, found at Bridgeness, now occupies a monumental position by the east side of Harbour Road.

ALISON COLLINGS PACING AT BRIDGENESS DISTANCE SLAB

Roman distance slabs recorded a completed length of building work, in Roman feet or Roman paces. In my picture, a demonstrative Alison Collings is busily pacing by the replica Bridgeness distance slab. A Roman pace was two of ours; so Romans went 'left-right-left'. A thousand of these Roman paces was one Roman Mile: *mille passus* from which our word 'mile' is derived. Here is something to think about: Your own single pace ('left-right') will be just under a yard and we have 1,760 yards to our mile. Does that sound about right?

When, eventually, our Antonine Trail delivers us to this end-of-the-Wall monument, we find the name of Antonine recorded in full with attached family names and those of predecessors, together with his rank and status including his piety: Imperator Caesar Titus Aelius Hadrianus Antoninus Augustus Pius. The letters 'PP' are short for 'Father of his Country'. The Legion doing the building work on this section of Wall was the II Augusta. There follows a record of the distance they completed, concluding with the abbreviation for 'they made it' 'FEC'.

Ordinary Building Stones and their Recycling

In my early Civil Engineering career, I had stone masons working for me. We Civil Engineers used a limited geological vocabulary, e.g. 'sandstone and slate', both sedimentary rocks used in building; or 'whin' which – at the risk of exasperating geologists – is a sort of grey, hard, (um) rocky rock. Whin resists wear and tear, so was used for carriageway setts and kerbstones. Confusingly, whin may be either hard sandstone or an igneous rock of volcanic origin. Our masons spent happy hours 'dressing' kerbstones. A rough-textured 'punched' whin was used for edging 'black-top' footways, but for a smoother surface adjacent to paving stones we specified 'nidged' whin which had a closely packed array of straight parallel grooves running across the width of the kerb. ('Nidge' is a Scots word, related to English 'nudge'.)

See if you can share the excitement of spotting examples of Roman masons' stone-dressing. I found examples at four locations, three of which we pass on our Antonine Trail. The Romans seemed to have minimised their efforts. If a stone could be cut with perfectly flat surfaces, no further dressing was required. Otherwise, a sort of 'nidging' system of parallel grooves was used. The grooves were spaced a centimetre or two apart and were cut diagonally (see the pictures). Sometimes, diagonal grooves were cut in two directions, covering the stone with criss-cross markings, cut diagonally, like a lop-sided noughts and crosses board.

I found strikingly similar examples across Scotland at Bearsden, Balmuildy, Castle Cary, and Cramond. At Bearsden Bathhouse the stones are *in situ*. The other examples have been recycled! At Balmuildy, the Trail crosses the River Kelvin. Thinking to photograph the (to me) alarmingly flat voussoir-arch stones while the bridge was still standing, I found – on later examining the results – that I had 'captured' Roman stones taken from nearby Balmuildy Fort. (Note: 'Voussoirs' are the arches of stone, forming the outer edges of the vault, or soffit, of a bridge. They are often segments of circles – or should be!)

At a cursory inspection of the forts at Castlecary and Cramond, I failed to see any criss-cross marked stones. But I found plenty in the medieval tower house of Castle Cary a kilometre south of the Roman fort site. I found more in Cramond Kirk, built and rebuilt on the site of the Roman Basilica in the centre of Cramond Fort.

In medieval times, the Livingston family blessed their good fortune – a free Roman stone quarry comprising the remains of Castlecary Fort. They carted their loot the kilometre southwards uphill to build their house of Castle Cary. 'Loot' is perhaps the wrong word: because the Fort was doubtless theirs in the first place. Because I am nosey, and to save you the bother, I took a trip up there and found the modern proprietor, Andrew Johnson busily restoring his magnificent property. Andrew kindly showed me some examples of Roman criss-crossed stones and allowed me to picture them. But he failed to show me his phallus! Romans sometimes placed stones, thus marked, as a talisman of fortune and fecundity. Andrew took me to look for the Castle Cary example, but the undergrowth defeated him: he had had more pressing restoration priorities. The Livingston looting was so thorough that, in the 1700s, Some antiquarians deduced, wrongly, that the Romans had actually built the tower house.

Cramond Fort seems to have been in Roman occupation for quite some time. There may have been an Agricolan Fort (*circa* 81 AD) on the site. The Antonine Fort dates from about 142 AD, but it was refurbished for a visit by Emperor Septimius Severus in 208 AD. I am not saying occupation was necessarily continuous. The site's importance was like a magnet for early Christians who built their church on the very site of the Cramond Roman Basilica or headquarters building. Not only did these Christians recycle Roman stones, some with criss-cross marks, but they recycled pagan beliefs. It seems to have helped faith and understanding to build early churches so that worshippers faced the Holy Land which was, conveniently, in the same direction in which sun-worshippers faced the rising sun. The ancient Romans had not thought through all the correct angles – they were aiming to overlook the River Forth – so the new Christian church needed new foundations, angled a bit differently. The rebuilding was therefore to an entirely new design, but recycled the old stones. Cramond Church (Kirk) has suffered several refurbishments. In 1910-11, an expansion effectively turned the congregation to face south (and the mid-day sun) and set some walls further out. We can now say that some Roman stones at Cramond have been recycled twice and some, just possibly, three times.

There now follows a picture essay on stones. See if you become cross-eyed.

STONES AT BEARSDEN BATH HOUSE

GROOVED STONES AT THE BATH HOUSE

FLAT 'ARCH' AT BALMORE ROAD BRIDGE OVER RIVER KELVIN

HERE ARE STONES FROM BALMUILDY ROMAN FORT

'CRISS-CROSS' STONE AT CASTLE CARY TOWER HOUSE

'CRISS-CROSS' STONE AT CRAMOND KIRK

'CRISS-CROSS' STONES IN THE WALL OF CASTLE CARY HOUSE

'CRISS-CROSS' STONES IN THE WALL OF CRAMOND KIRK

A four-page picture summary of the Trail now follows

INTRODUCTORY DAY: PATH BY GRUGGIE'S BURN

DAY ONE: GRUFFALO ENCOUNTER BY KILMARDINNY LOCH

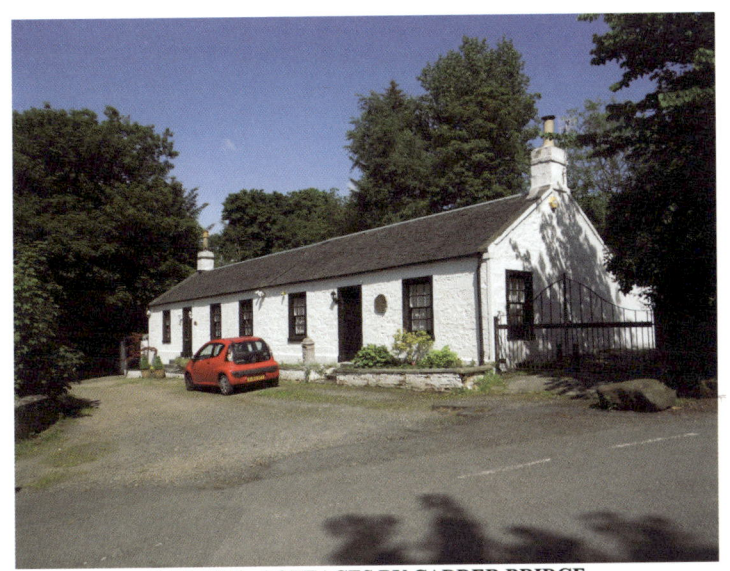

DAY TWO: COTTAGES BY CADDER BRIDGE

DAY THREE: LUGGIE ACQUEDUCT

DAY FOUR: RAMPART, BERM, AND DITCH ABOVE FALKIRK WHEEL

DAY FIVE: PASSING MUMRILLS FORT SITE (right)

DAY SIX: BRIDGENESS TOWER AND THE WALL'S END BOWLING GREEN

EXTRA DAY: RIVER ALMOND AT CRAMOND

X) VOTE HERE: IS IT WORTH THE WALK?

The trouble is: if you build walls with squashy earth or turf, and you dig ditches and holes, and then abandon the whole enterprise for nearly two thousand years – you expect some deterioration.

When the Romans built their Wall, farmers must have gone ape at the cutting of a great swathe through their property, severing land in the north from land in the south. It must have seemed to them as we see a new motorway or high-speed train line. Apart from the loss of land, probably without compensation, you would have found that to get from your house north of the Wall to your fields in the sunny south, you might well have had to pay the Romans a toll. If you demurred, you'd be told off; or, more likely, cut down – literally – to size.

So, what happened after the Wall was abandoned? Once you were sure the Romans had really gone, you grabbed back the land. Buildings were not much use: the Romans had dismantled or burnt them. Pity about the dearth of reusable stone (most buildings, bar stone foundations, were wooden). As we found in Section (9), at the stone fort of Castlecary, the Livingstone family nicked the stones for their tower house; whilst at Cramond, the Church has identifiable stones dressed by Roman masons in its walls.

You will notice when we are walking the Trail that sections of Wall and Ditch are best preserved where the planting of crops was not viable; on sloping or wooded ground, for instance. Where there are modern field systems, they tell us the Roman Wall and Ditch remains have been "ploughed out". Yeah, right! If it had been me trying to recoup land my father or grandfather had lost to Roman construction teams, I'd have called my pals round and we'd have worked our socks off shoving and shovelling the dreaded Wall into its equally dreaded Ditch. We are talking about getting back a strip of land 20 or 30 metres wide, and if we include the area to, and including, the Military Road, we are talking about getting back a strip perhaps 100 metres wide. That's a lot of barley! This, to me, explains why some lengths of Wall have now but a gentle dip, in cross section, as we scan along the line. I would suggest that, *after* the basic land reclamation work, *then* they 'ploughed out' the Wall.

With ploughed-out Wall and vanquished forts, is it worth the walk?

Yes! Let's run (mentally, at least) along the route:

If you do the optional **Introductory Day,** you will be able to start Wall Day One after breakfast on *your* second day. The introductory visit to Dumbarton Castle will allow you to stand where our inquisitive and observant Romans must have stood, checking boats in their harbour and ensuring the natives were behaving.

On **Wall Day One,** you can start from Milton after yesterday's stroll. If you have just arrived this morning, you can begin your adventure from Bowling train station and walk along to Old Kilpatrick Fort at the start of the Wall with really nothing to see there. But when you wander down near to the bank of the River Clyde, it evokes a picture of Romans standing here where, they say, was the furthest downstream point for fording the river at low tide. It is *still* the furthest downstream river crossing, via the Erskine Bridge which superseded the Erskine Ferry. As we've discovered, the Romans continued their military road westwards from this Fort. Drink in the atmosphere. Two kilometres along the Forth and Clyde Canal which tends to accompany the Wall as far as Falkirk, we divert via Parkhall Golf Course to the site of Duntocher Fort, which seems to have superseded an earlier fortlet. All you can see is an outline of some walling below the grass and a mere hint of ditch(es). But you can appreciate the outlook the Romans got. We pass Cleddans where a fortlet stood. Why are there farm buildings on the *same* site? If we take my diversion to Castle Hill Fort site, you really can appreciate how the Romans must have felt superior here. This fort has not been excavated. Bearsden Fort reveals its bath-house. The rest of the fort is below suburbia.

On **Wall Day Two,** as we approach Balmuildy Fort from the north, we may consider how the Romans bridged the River Kelvin. Their legacy lives on: the modern Balmore Road chooses much the same crossing point. One day, perhaps, Balmuildy Farm may be turned into a visitor centre when, we may hope, foundations of the fort will be revealed – once more – to view. Back on the Forth and Clyde Canal for a good six kilometres, we can look up at the site of Cadder Fort across the canal, and we pass a fortlet site across the canal at Glasgow Bridge. Kirkintilloch Roman Fort, with the name meaning 'the fort at the end of the ridge' has a great outlook north. It was taken over as a medieval peel tower before lapsing into a modern municipal park, complete with a fountain in the form of Faustina. That was the name of Antonine's wife: their daughter's name, too.

FAUSTINA, ANTONINE'S DAUGHTER, KIRKINTILLOCH

Wall Day Three takes us on, or close to, another five kilometres of canal, passing the site of Auchendavy Fort – again occupied by farm buildings. Later, our spirits rise, as do we, as we head up to Bar Hill Fort with its consolidated remains and another bath house foundation. This fort was the most elevated on the Antonine Wall. On your way up to this fort you will be accompanying a most obvious Antonine Ditch. From Bar Hill, going down and later going up again, we find dramatic Ditch and evidence of Wall, too, as we pass over Croy Hill where the site of the Fort can be hard to detect. On our way to Westerwood Fort we pass quite spectacular ditch-works. This fort, again, invited farm buildings to occupy a corner of the site. The farm is now (2013) abandoned and it is also an abandoned youth centre. The modern invasion here is by golfers.

On **Wall Day Four** you can, if you divert, see Castlecary Fort site with some stone foundations in a group of trees beside the railway line which bisects the site. The Wall and canal now go neck and neck for 4 km to Bonnybridge, passing Seabegs Wood with a fortlet site just west of the wood. Leaving our canal to visit Rough Castle, we find almost 4 km of dramatic Ditch and some clearly visible Wall. Rough Castle Fort is really worth the visit. I think Ditches here were cleared in the early nineteen hundreds, for our benefit. Watling Lodge Fortlet site is now occupied, sadly, by Watling Lodge; but the adjoining sections of Ditch are well looked after by Historic Scotland.

LOOKING WEST TO WATLING LODGE ALONG THE NORTHERN UPCAST MOUND. VERY COMPRESSED RAMPART SEEN ON LEFT

On **Wall Day Five** (which those in a hurry can combine with Wall Day Four) we start by checking another rather secret Ditch length at

Bantaskine before taking a dramatic detour to dodge central Falkirk. Where *was* Falkirk Fort? Arnothill, perhaps. Now we're on the Union Canal and passing through Falkirk Canal Tunnel (using its footway!) and over Callendar Wood Hill to visit Callendar House with its museum and tea room. We pass the site of Mumrills Fort, the largest Wall fort at nearly 3 hectares (7 acres), though its foundations lie out of sight below a field. It held cavalry.

Our final **Wall Day: Six,** after another detour dodges the M9 motorway, we visit a final section of Wall and Ditch at Polmont Woods before we pass Inveravon Fort site (farm) with nothing to see. A walk along a road built in the Ditch has us wondering what was wrong with the Military Way, before we find the neatly pegged and labelled Kinneil Fortlet site. If your walk is finishing today, you will want to take souvenir pictures by the new (2012) monument in Harbour Road, Bo'ness, which marks the end of the Antonine Wall (perhaps). If you started at Bowling you will end at a bowling green!

The **Extra Day,** walking the shore path to Cramond is recommended. Carriden Fort site is mostly a house (B&B) and garden, now. Later, the delights of Blackness Castle, Abercorn Church, and the village of Queensferry await you. Cramond Fort, beyond the Wall, has more building foundations visible than any other Antonine Wall site and it may one day be getting a visitor centre. If you haven't got into the Roman mind set by now, you never will.

VOTE NOW! Let's organise our Roamin' Holiday!

ABERCORN CHURCH

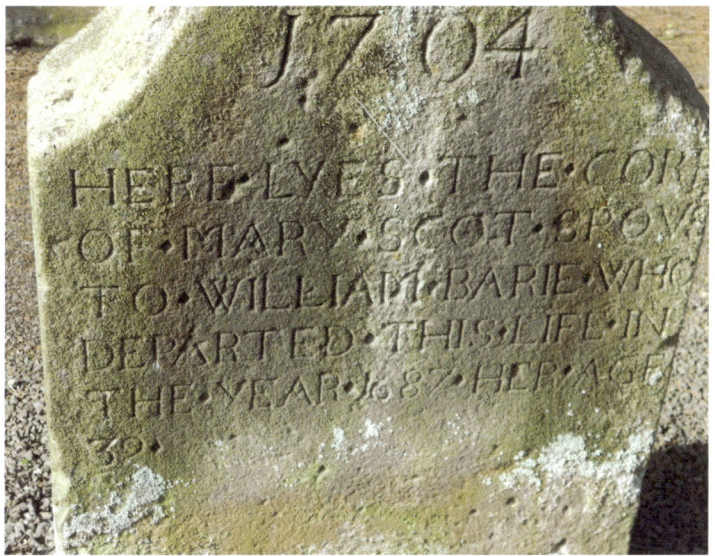

HERE.LYES.THE.CORP/OF.MARY.SCOT.SPOUS.TO.WILLIAM.BARIE.
WHO/DEPARTED.THIS.LIFE.IN/THE YEAR.1687.HER.AGE.39.

PART TWO

PART TWO

ROAMIN'

AN ANTONINE TRAIL
    'Full Trail' distance: 124.5 km (77 miles)
    'Wall Days Only' distance: 91 km (56 miles)

Important Note
In planning your walk, decide whether you are tackling the *Full* Antonine Trail, a maximum of 8 days with the distance above. Or, are you to do the *Wall Days Only* (excluding introductory and extra days), a maximum of 6 days with a distance of 91 km (56 miles)?

    The book's sub-heading hinted at a coast-to-coast walk. You *shall walk coast-to-coast* with the Full Trail *or* by doing the Wall Days Only!

(Numbers in brackets in the text correspond to the same numbers on the maps for each walking day.)

DAILY DISTANCES, AND O.S. MAPS

- Full Trail days have a Berger dot.
  Wall Days Only have distances marked with an asterisk *

	Km	**(miles)**
• Introductory Day: To Milton	5	(3)
• Wall Day One: To Bearsden	20	(12)
{If starting at Bowling Station}	18.5*	(11)*
• Wall Day Two: To Kirkintilloch	16*	(10)*
• Wall Day Three: To Castlecary	16*	(10)*
• Wall Day Four: To Falkirk	14.5*	(9)*
• Wall Day Five: To Beancross	12*	(7½)*
{Combine Days 4 & 5; omit side visits}	20	(12)
• Wall Day Six: To Carriden	16	(10)
{To end of Wall in Harbour Road}	14*	(8½)*
• Extra Day: To Cramond	25	(15½)
{If cheating by hopping on the bus}	15.5	(9½)
• Full Trail distance	124.5	(77)
Wall Days Only distance	91*	(56)*

Ordnance Survey Maps:
You can supplement <u>this book's excellent walking maps</u> with Ordnance Survey maps: *Landranger 1:50,000 scale sheets 64 and 65 cover the entire route.* Alternatively, Explorer 1:25,000 scale sheets 342, 347, 348, 349, and 350 can be used. (347 has only the introductory day; 348 has but a single mile not included on other sheets; 350 has only the Extra Day to Cramond.) *So, 'Wall Days Walkers' need only sheets 342 and 349.*

The text, which follows, fully explains all your options.

AN INTRODUCTORY DAY: WEST OF THE WALL

DUMBARTON EAST STATION TO MILTON (TRAVEL LODGE): 5 km (3 miles)

Note:
Since not many of you happen to live at Bowling (where there is a railway station and where the Forth and Clyde canal begins – or ends) or at neighbouring Old Kilpatrick (where The Antonine Wall ends – or begins) we shall have to make allowance for walkers to arrive here.

While we are waiting, we can start with a spelling lesson: The written record suggests that errors crept in, in the past, and are now lovingly cherished and preserved. We should note that the town is Du**m**barton, with an 'm', but the county is Du**n**bartonshire, with an 'n'. Do not mix these up, or your 'error' may be pointed out. Do not bother to mention that the usual word in Scotland for a fortification on a hill is/was **dun**. Do not ask about the oddly spelt 'barton' when the thing was once the dun of the 'Britons', and don't even *think* about querying the tautological addition of 'Castle'.

As you'll have deduced, we're starting with a visit to Dumbarton Castle. The Romans had built a road parallel to The Antonine Wall and then continued this road westwards from the west end of the Wall at what we now call Old Kilpatrick, so we may be certain the Romans were at Dumbarton Castle which also benefitted from a harbour. Although – since the Britons *hadn't* got there by the time of the Romans (or perhaps I should suggest that the locals had not yet been identified as Britons) – it was, in those days, referred to as the Rock of the Clyde, or Alt Clut in local-speak.

Let's walk! Use the map.
Our walk begins at Dumbarton East Station because it is served by trains from Glasgow and Edinburgh. Check the *detailed*

timetable to find which trains stop here. If you go on to Dumbarton Central Station, you'll have to walk back about one kilometre.

Emerge from Dumbarton East Station onto Glasgow Road. From the station exit, cross Glasgow Road and turn *left* (east). Cross the mouth of a side road (Buchanan Street) and also cross a bridge over a stream. Then, *immediately* turn right onto paving slabs which lead to a path along the bank of the stream which runs parallel to Buchanan Street. I believe the stream is Gruggies Burn which helps drain run-off from the Kilpatrick Hills into the River Clyde.

At the end of the path, turn right and – in 150m – at a *crossroads* – turn left into Castle Road, but noting a take-away here 'Young's Corner Shop'. Go down Castle Road to visit Dumbarton Castle. Today's lazy schedule should allow plenty time for this activity. The Castle is in the care of Historic Scotland who make a modest entrance charge for non members or those without reciprocal membership: English Heritage membership for instance. The only sign at the Castle entrance says 'No Parking' and we have to go through the entrance arch to find out where we've got to!

ON TOP OF THE DUN OF THE BRITONS

The map, below, is the first of our large scale walking maps. Since our introductory day has only 5 km (3 miles), we have decided to show the map-symbols key at the right hand side. As you move on to the use of the other walking Trail maps, please bear in mind that the map-symbols are to be found only on this map on this page.

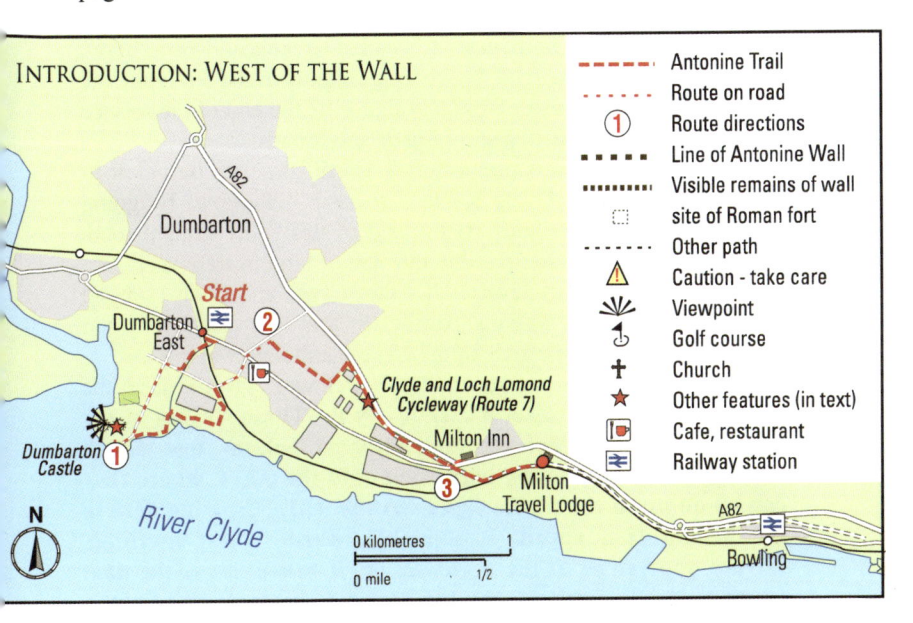

INTRODUCTION: WEST OF THE WALL

Map key:
- Antonine Trail
- Route on road
- ① Route directions
- Line of Antonine Wall
- Visible remains of wall
- site of Roman fort
- Other path
- ⚠ Caution - take care
- Viewpoint
- Golf course
- ✝ Church
- ★ Other features (in text)
- Cafe, restaurant
- Railway station

(1) On leaving the Castle, cross the road to follow signs 'Dumbarton Foreshore Walkway'. (You may earlier have seen a sign 'The Castle Circular Path'.) This takes us by the shore of the River Clyde until we have to cross a footbridge over Gruggies Burn – near its mouth (see map). Bear right here to continue, with the Clyde on our right. (It can flood at very high tide.) Soon, when we get the opportunity to turn left at a fork in the path – leaving the River Clyde at our backs – we do so. Perhaps I shouldn't mention the sewage works now on our right. We presently pass a staggered barrier to join a quiet road, but noisy if a train is on the railway on our right. Turn right at a junction, go under a railway bridge, round

a curve – we're on National Cycle Route no. 7 – and pass a fire station (left) before crossing the A814 Glasgow Road at traffic signals (Note: at the north-east corner of this junction is a 'Keystore' which sells food and soft drinks. Attached to it is a café, 'Benvenuti' – Italian for 'Welcome' (apt, don't you think?) – where the café/restaurant symbol is shown on our map, Benvenuti is recommended for soup, sandwiches, and so forth.) Continue, via the side road heading north east. It's called Greenhead Road. Soon, take the quiet service road by bearing slightly right. (Avoid the 'main' road which rises to cross a bridge.) At the end of the service road, we find ourselves at a sort of path 'crossroads'.

(2) Turn right and continue for ½ km till the path turns left to join a road. Follow Cycle Route 7 towards 'Glasgow' by going right and immediately left. At the end of this short straight road, 'Third Avenue', and after passing the side of large warehouses, turn right at the Route 7 cycleway. It's the 'Clyde and Loch Lomond Cycleway'. We are walking parallel to the busy A82 (left) and passing (right) the gable ends of the afore-mentioned warehouses.

(3) In 1 km, after passing the last warehouse, we see ahead the A814 bridge which crosses the Trail. **(N.B. Those staying at the Milton Inn, which I can recommend, must look for, and take, a short gravelly connecting path *right* onto the A814, where they can go on up to the traffic signals at the A82. Crossing here to the Milton Inn, ahead, is straightforward. Next morning, retrace your steps to the cycleway or, if brave, cross the dual carriageway in front of the Inn to take the footpath directly opposite and then turn left on reaching the cycleway. The postcode and phone number of the Inn are G82 2TD and 01389 761 401).** Otherwise, continue on the cycle route *under* the A814 and past a cross path. This introductory walk ends at Milton Travelodge, ¾ km (½ mile) further, where the Trail is sandwiched between the railway (right) and our Travelodge (left) – entrance round the front! (Postcode and phone number are G82 2TZ and 01389 765 202).

ENTRANCE TO DUMBARTON CASTLE

NOW THERE FOLLOW SIX 'WALL DAYS'

WALL DAY ONE
MILTON (TRAVEL LODGE)
TO BEARSDEN (PREMIER INN): 20 km (12 miles)
OR
BOWLING (TRAIN STATION)
TO BEARSDEN (PREMIER INN): 18.5 km (11 miles)

Note:
From Bowling Station we soon come to Bowling Boat Basin – within metres of the Forth and Clyde Canal's sea lock which allows boats to gain access to the river. Then *within one kilometre,* we come to the beginning of The Antonine Wall. Can this proximity be a coincidence? Well, no, actually! Both construction efforts, although separated by some sixteen hundred years, were influenced by the depth of the River Clyde. The Roman Wall had to protect the empire against intruders fording the river at low tide – there was no river dredging, in those days. The canal had to ensure boats met deep enough water to float in when they entered the river.

Unless you start the day with a picnic lunch in your backpack, you'll pick something up at Mountblow "Superstore" or you'll grab a bite at West Park Hotel (see text).

At Golden Hill, Duntocher, you will catch the general idea of what it is like to visit a Roman fort in our own day and age. The topography remains the same, so we have to concentrate on the *outlook*. We, later, utilise a goodly stretch of improved woodland footpaths to bring us close to Bearsden. And we must thank my late grandmother who lived there – in Bearsden, not in the woods – for my close grasp of pedestrian routes to lead us to the end of our day.

Let's walk! Use the map.
From the start of the section at Milton Travel Lodge, regain the cycleway – which passes behind it – and go left (east). Shortly, we cross the A814 on the level across the south arm of a roundabout, using the nearby crossing, if required. Continue towards Bowling on the cycle route.

To start your walk if arriving at Bowling Station by train, go up past the Railway Inn (right) – 'food served all day' it says – and continue. Cross the main road and walk up steps and a rough path to turn right on the cycleway and to go through a short tunnel.

THE SHORT TUNNEL, LOOKING WESTWARDS

Otherwise, the cycle route goes under the short tunnel, passing a waterfall (left), then along a narrow strip of public park, across a signalled crossing of the A814, and past a sign 'Welcome to Bowling Basin'. Then we cross a bridge over a *live* railway and curve left. Just *past* a junction (with a road which doubles back right), go right to cross a bascule footbridge over the canal and past

'Magic Cycles' (2012), (right). Walk up past two canal basins (left) containing moored boats.

(1) Follow the towpath, soon with the Erskine Bridge seen ahead high above the River Clyde. The western end of the Antonine Wall will not be apparent to you (cries of disappointment): but look out for a road sloping down towards the opposite canal bank. The terminal Roman Fort was across the canal from a hut and a footpath (right) which our Trail passes. If you're nosey, cross the convenient Ferrydyke bascule bridge over the canal and see the site of Old Kilpatrick Fort in front of you, fenced off and with some sort of modern industrial installation on top of it. More interesting for us is to nip down towards the River Clyde by the path opposite the canal bridge, noting ruined stables which were built to house canal barge horses. Here, over a wall, we get a great view of Erskine Bridge and we are standing near the spot where the Roman soldiers will have looked upstream and downstream, checking that all was well and dreaming, perhaps, of how far they were from home. The Antonine Wall ran down to the river's edge. The fort seems to have pre-dated the wall and may originally have been the location of an Agricolan fort.

(You may skip this paragraph! Here we are at the start of the Wall and already I am going to indicate a closer-to-the-Wall route [see Part One] than *we* are going to follow, and why we are choosing *our* route. So: here is the 'closer' route which I AM <u>NOT</u> ADVOCATING. I confess it is safe; it's just boring – I've checked! One could, from Old Kirkpatrick Fort make one's way on dull streets east then north to the A814, thence making one's way up the road past Kilpatrick Railway Station and under the A82 dual carriageway till one meets a footpath heading east and located just north of the eastbound 'on' slip-road. This takes one up past a cemetery to the 'Beeches' path which follows the Wall line for a kilometre before continuing on road through Duntocher still [partly] on the Wall line for another kilometre before one reaches the A810 and turning left, and soon right to find Golden Hill Park.)

Since *no one* can follow the line of the Wall for at least the first mile, we – sensible Trail-blazers – continue along the canal tow path, under the Erskine Bridge and past 'Lock 37'. On our towpath, we cross a road (which itself crosses the canal on a swing bridge) and which once took traffic down to a jetty to cross the River Clyde on the Erskine Ferry, until the road bridge opened in 1971.

Wall Day 1: Milton to Bearsden

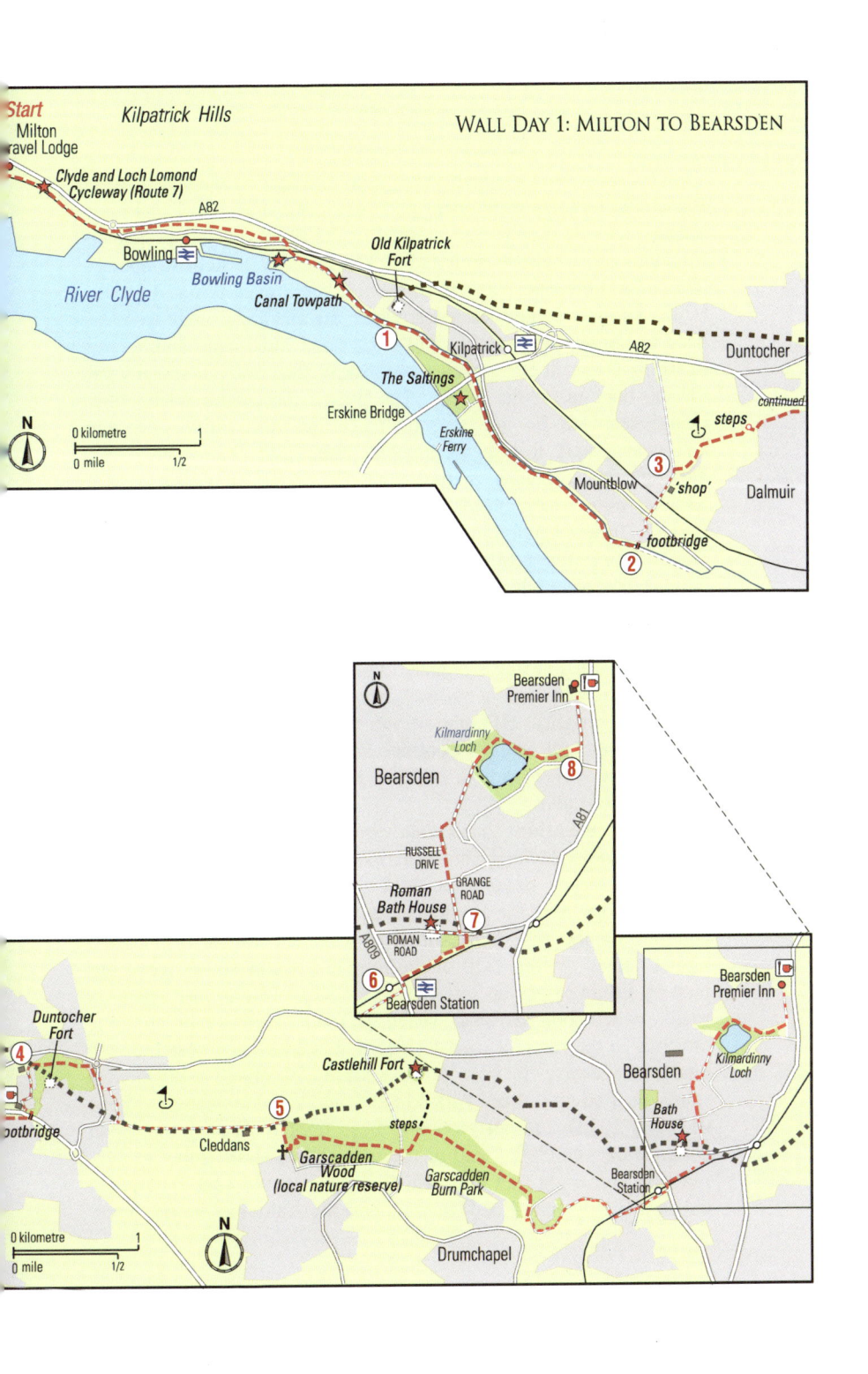

Start
Milton Travel Lodge
Kilpatrick Hills
Clyde and Loch Lomond Cycleway (Route 7)
A82
Bowling
River Clyde
Bowling Basin
Canal Towpath
Old Kilpatrick Fort
①
The Saltings
Erskine Bridge
Kilpatrick
A82
Duntocher
Erskine Ferry
Mountblow
③
'shop'
steps
continued
Dalmuir
footbridge
②

N
0 kilometre 1
0 mile ½

Duntocher Fort
④
footbridge
Cleddans
Castlehill Fort
⑤
steps
Garscadden Wood (local nature reserve)
Garscadden Burn Park
Bearsden Station
Bearsden
Bath House
Kilmardinny Loch
Bearsden Premier Inn
Drumchapel

Bearsden (inset)
Kilmardinny Loch
Bearsden
RUSSELL DRIVE
GRANGE ROAD
Roman Bath House
⑦
ROMAN ROAD
A809
⑥
Bearsden Station
A81
⑧
Bearsden Premier Inn
N

0 kilometre 1
0 mile ½
N

Don't expect to see much canal boat traffic. At present (2013) British Waterways staff open all bridges and operate all locks for boaters who, if they're accustomed to the do-it-yourself system in England, can't believe their luck. For the DIY system to operate here, a lot more cash needs to be spent to make everything fit for use by the public. Some lock gates, which are currently tough to open, need to operate more freely and boats need canal-side landing and boarding points at every bridge and lock so the crew can actually get off the boat to do the work. The present maximum traffic flow would seem to be one or two boats per day, only, since the waterways staff follow the punters (sorry) in their vans. So, although the reopening of the canal, after years of disuse, cost a fortune, more really needs to be done. A good kilometre past Erskine Bridge, a pylon line crosses high over the canal.

(2) Soon, after gentle right and left bends, we come to another bascule bridge at which we turn left to cross the canal. We go up the road for about 100m and at the top we go right. Our quiet road curves left but soon – at a church (right) – we bear right to cross the main A814 road at traffic signals. On we go, northwards and, once we have crossed over a railway, we pass the small "Mountblow Superstore" (right). (If some of you want to get stuff for a picnic, the rest of us will wait!) Continue *across the mouth of* Littleholm Place (right, which leads to LARGE HOMES in the shape of three tall blocks of flats).

(3) **Pay attention:** *Immediately past a parking area (right), turn right passing a bollard,* into a narrow path which runs parallel to Littleholm Place. Beyond the third block of flats, Clyde Court, we cross a bridge over the Duntocher Burn and – ignoring junctions – continue on the now hedge-lined path up the middle of Parkhall Golf Course. At the TOP of the rise, at a signpost, we leave our path by turning right up a few concrete steps. Here, turn left on a road – which soon narrows. When the road widens again, continue onwards to the ramp of a footbridge which takes us across the A82 dual carriageway. In front of us, 8.5 km (5½ miles) from today's start, we find the West Park Hotel (food/accommodation; phone 01389 872333). If not stopping, bear right – passing the Hotel entrance on your left – and at the foot of this short slope, at a T-junction, turn right (it's Old Mill Road) and at the next T-junction, turn left (it's Roman Road) to walk past the Antonine Sports Centre

(no café, no food, no coffee machine, but the name sounds encouraging).

(4) Immediately past the Centre's exit (on our left), we turn right through the gates of Golden Hill Park to follow a sign 'Antonine Wall and Roman Fort'. Yes! Duntocher Roman Fort was built on the top of this hill we face. Now we must go to the top *up the zig-zag path*, stopping to examine what we find in a small fenced enclosure (left) by the path. The Antonine Wall climbed straight up this steep slope to the fort at the top. The Romans built their turf wall on a 4.5m wide stone foundation. Here we see the dressed kerb stones at each side of the wall, with other stones placed by hand to fill the gap in between. Other Roman turf walls don't seem to have had the stone base; for instance, the western length of Hadrian's Wall was originally of turf but *without* a stone base. So the Antonine Wall had a design innovation. What did it achieve? (1) It helped control the wall's dimensions so rookies could get on with cutting and setting the turf blocks. (2) It stopped the turf blocks slipping, especially here! (3) It permitted drainage channels and culverts to be led under the wall.

Past the fenced enclosure we find an information plaque, but we carry on up to pass the end of a hedge (left). Just go left with the final zig-zag till we come to another plaque, showing the fort layout. At this plaque, we *turn right* up the grass area, keeping that rough grass – on the line of the Antonine Wall – on our right.

> Note: Between us and a concrete triangulation pillar (trig point), we may detect a slight hollow: the Antonine Ditch. In fact there was, unusually, a double ditch along the front of this fort. On our right (or behind our backs if we're surveying the ditch(es)) is a 20m square fortlet, to which was later *added* the larger fort – just past the fortlet, as we walk slowly by. Both the fortlet and the fort, seemingly, pre-date the arrival of the Wall. Ah, that would explain the double ditch then, since double or triple ditches often protected forts on sides which were *not* adjacent to the Antonine Wall. (A later annexe, added to the north east of the fort, enclosed the old fortlet within its bounds.)

When we have finished our inspection of the fort outline and taken in the views from the trig point, noticing – perhaps – Castle Hill to the east (see below), we rejoin the path on which we arrived, bearing right to follow the continuing path downhill (ignoring path junctions) until we come to a car park which we continue through, to arrive at a road, near a roundabout. Turn right down the service road for over 100m to a signalled pedestrian crossing. Cross the road here. On the other side, turn right, then left, down footpath steps to join a street (Cleddans Crescent). Turn first right; then bear slightly left. Keep going to the end of houses at a T-junction where we turn left into Cleddans Road (street sign).

Well: we are truly walking the Wall, now! Our Trail exactly follows the Wall for over a kilometre as it slowly, and then more rapidly, rises as we near Cleddans Farm. As we pass a barrier at the end of the public stretch of road, look to our left: If the slim, upright tree across the field had been there when the Romans were here it would have reminded them of the slim, upright trees back home. Only thing is: it's *not* a tree. It's a cunningly disguised radio mast. The Trail and, indeed, the Wall go straight past Cleddans – now a horse-riding centre but at the site of a Roman fortlet. Beyond the farm we lose height and pass a barrier gate till, in the valley we stop by a ford and an Irish bridge (a stream in pipes). Here we part company with the Antonine Wall. *Its* course veers somewhat left, uphill in a field, where we cannot follow. It is heading for Castle Hill (not visible from here) where there was a fort.

(At the ford, three counties meet: we are leaving West Dunbartonshire and entering The City of Glasgow, whilst East Dunbartonshire contains Castle Hill.)

(5) We cross the Irish bridge, or the ford, and turn right here to walk downhill. Just past a basketball court (right) and *before* a building presently (2012) housing Drumchapel Baptist Church, we turn left to enter Garscadden Wood and Local Nature Reserve on an 'official' path which immediately curves left and soon zig-zags back uphill. We may see, but not step in, the evidence of horses from Cleddans enjoying our Trail. We may see planes coming in low to land at Glasgow Airport; (take-offs are higher in the sky). Eventually we are slowly descending. At an official path junction, we go straight on. At a second official path junction, bear left and if we LOOK LEFT we get a view on the horizon of Castle Hill, site of the next Roman Fort on the Antonine Wall. The path soon takes us, via a zig-zag, down to a road (Peel Glen Road). Go right round the railing to cross the road carefully and enter the continuing path through Garscadden Burn Park.

Our Trail goes straight uphill, ignoring a grit path (right). We go under two pylon lines and soon curve right. **Very soon we notice a narrow trodden path which goes up steps (left).**

> If the weather is fine and you have time – allow half an hour to an hour – I recommend a there-and-back side trip to visit Castle Hill Roman Fort site and I have included this in today's distance calculation (1 km or ¾ mile). Go up the steps and continue on the trodden route. This path really goes up to the farm (more stables), located to the right of the hilltop. So we shall have to fork left: But we must wait until we are up in clear grassland and can *see* the tree-girt summit. Fork left here where we can see the trodden way heading towards the summit (see photo).

FORK LEFT HERE

> The fort reminds one of square pegs and round holes. These stick-to-the-correct-procedure Romans tried to fit their standard squarish fort onto a circular hilltop. You may well blunder over the two-thousand-year-old defence ditches as you come up to the top. Consulting our maps will indicate which overgrown hedge accompanies the line of the Antonine Ditch as it comes up the hill from the west. We can look down on the fields where the Wall diverted off the line of that track past Cleddans farm. It is *really* hard to be sure where the Wall ran. (If you think you could wander off

through Bearsden from here; yes, you could. But our Trail is simply better!) So, enjoy the views before returning down the hill and down the steps.

FROM THE LIGHT GREEN FIELD, LEFT OF THE TOP OF THE PYLON, A TRACE OF THE HOLLOW OF THE ANTONINE DITCH CURVES DOWN TOWARDS THE DARK BUSHES ON THE LEFT OF THE PHOTO.
FROM THE TOP OF CASTLE HILL

On reaching the foot of the steps, we turn left to resume our Trail on the official path. At an official path junction we go ahead and, after a substantial straightish section, at another official path junction we again go ahead – on the higher route. At the next junction we again go ahead as we slowly lose altitude. Soon, as we curve right, we are passing a vast electricity substation (or is it a *main* station?) on our right, and we are aware of a road up to our left. Soon we meet a side road where we turn left and, on the 'main' road, turn right. This is called – perhaps unexpectedly – Station Road. Soon the flat expanse of Colquhoun Park (playing fields) opens out, (and we have *come out of* The City of Glasgow once more). Presently, the road splits. The left (upper) route serves houses numbers 54 to 42. Take either route: they join up after 150 m. As we pass a playing-field car-parking area on our right, our road is curving right, slightly wider now. We go under a railway bridge. Station Road goes left and in ½ km we come to Bearsden Station. There is an inn here (with refreshments including food) called 'The Inn' (tel: 0141 942 6752, and postcode G61 4AN). We are 2.5 km (1¾ miles) from our Premier Inn.

(6) Go left on the main road, Drymen Road A809, and cross the road at the signalled crossing located on top of the bridge over the railway line. On the far side of the road, go left, but *immediately right* down a narrow path going beside the railway. Now, ignoring a path (on the left), we walk on to pass houses and then tennis courts. When our confined route is paralleled (on the left) by a vehicle lane, we should change to the left hand side to join the vehicle lane. This curves left and soon joins Roman Road which is believed to be a *real* Roman road lying on top of the Roman military way which ran the full length of the Antonine Wall. Turn left on Roman Road, passing the mouth of Grange Road (right) and continuing for a short distance. Just beyond flats (right), we find an open space (also right) behind the roadside trees. Here we enter the gate to the Bearsden Roman Bath House which served the soldiers here, at Bearsden Roman Fort on the Antonine Wall. Real Roman remains, at last! Roman Road bisects the Fort site.

(7) Leave by the gate you entered and retrace your steps, to turn left into the afore-mentioned Grange Road. At the T-junction at the top of Grange Road, *go ahead on the continuing footpath – in the same northerly direction.* This comes down to join a road, Russell Drive, where we go ahead, still maintaining the same direction and ignoring side roads. When, in about 150 m and over a rise, Russell Drive turns left, WE DO NOT! We go straight forward into a *very* short cul-de-sac and take another continuing footpath. **Immediately behind the house on our right, turn right** then curve left and, in 30 m, we have to turn right, soon coming to a road, turning left, stepping past house no. *'thirty nine'*, and walking to the end of the road, again ignoring side roads until, continuing on a footpath, we head straight past Kilmardinny Loch (on our right) following the main path and bearing right to avoid steps. (Please read the note about the loch on the next page.) Beyond a widened seating area, bear left, gently upwards and away from the water, to a small car park where we again bear left to walk with houses on our left.

(8) Finally, our path emerges from trees to a grassy area and joins a road (Burnbrae Avenue). Turn left and walk to the end of the road at a T-junction (210 m). Cross straight over and continue ahead down a short lane (sign: Burnbrae 2 mins), where we find steps leading down to the entrance to the Bearsden Premier Inn, 279 Milngavie Road, Lanarkshire, G61 3DQ. 'The Burnbrae' restaurant is next door, just downhill (tel: 0141 942 5951).

Kilmardinny Loch: My official Trail goes straight past Kilmardinny Loch, as described; but it is perhaps a little prettier to go round the loch to the right via the far side. Here you will pass some chain-saw carvings by sculptor Iain Chalmers and a Gruffalo by Julia Donaldson; see website (chainsawcreations.co.uk).

THAT'S THE END OF OUR FIRST 'WALL DAY'. FIVE TO GO!

WALL DAY TWO
BEARSDEN (PREMIER INN)
TO KIRKINTILLOCH (SMITH'S HOTEL): 16 km (10 miles)

Note:
Yesterday, we started on The Antonine Wall with a sight of the site of **Old Kilpatrick Fort**. Today we *avoid* **New Kilpatrick**, the cemetery with two well preserved, exposed sections of Wall base. My decision was to keep you safe from fast road traffic. Our route utilises part of the Kelvin Walkway and more of our Forth and Clyde Canal. Any attempt by us to follow the line of the Wall more closely would stand a good chance of offering us up as road-kill! Balmuildy Road is not exactly a pedestrian's paradise although it is close to (and partly on) the Wall; and so we have avoided it. We do take a stroll up Balmore Road which, fortunately, does have a footway.

Our Trail has some excellent refreshment stop opportunities: Dobbie's Garden Centre for morning coffee, Bishopbriggs' Leisuredrome for lunch, and later – perhaps – the Stables at Glasgow Bridge (see text). We get back on the exact line of the Wall on approaching the Roman Fort site at Kirkintilloch.

Let's walk! Use the map.
From the Bearsden Premier Inn, we walk down to the main road, A81, passing 'The Burnbrae'. Turn left on the A81. At the roundabout go *straight* ahead (sign: Town Centre). Soon we pass another Premier Inn (right) – the Milngavie one. Also, we pass a Police Station and then we turn right, where there's a letter box on the corner, into Keystone Road. I bet they call the local constabulary the Keystone Cops – well, they will now! Keystone Road curves left: go to the end where we turn right (sign: 'Allander Way' Glasgow 6). **(Note: We are ½ mile from Milngavie Town Centre's start of the West Highland Way. To go there one would take the footpath ahead, where signed.)** We Antonine

Trailers are now down at the main road, A81, where we turn left under a railway bridge.

(1) At the traffic lights, turn right to cross the road and go through a gate to a footpath (sign: Allander Way). We are now following the Allander Water. Our path crosses the Water on a bridge – so we are kept out of Douglas Park Golf Course on the opposite bank (right). After the golf course, a bridge takes us back to the right bank.

(2) After nearly 2 km on the path, our Trail rises up to an aqueduct which carries some of Glasgow's water supply – it's in a pipe. Do NOT attempt to continue on the river bank! (The river path is a bit overgrown, downstream). *Our* Trail turns right through a pedestrian gate to follow the aqueduct for a few metres to the road. **(Opposite, if we cross CAREFULLY, we find The Tickled Trout Restaurant with – up behind it – a Dobbie's Garden Centre (tel: 01360 620721), with coffee shop and restaurant. The line of the Antonine Wall runs directly behind Dobbie's. It is long since ploughed out – i.e. flat – but Dobbie's have recreated a short length of replica Wall and Ditch out the back of their centre building, beside the play area. After your visit, re-cross the road CAREFULLY and turn right down the roadside footway.)** If not visiting Dobbie's, simply turn left down the roadside footway. A few metres before the next bridge over the Allander Water and opposite a roundabout sign, find a gap in the hedge, right, by a tall pole bearing a disc. Cross here CAREFULLY, go through the gap and, surprise, surprise, we're on tarmac! It's the old road and it leads us to a neat pedestrian route by forking left under the A879, Balmore Road; a good spot for bird watching, kingfishers for instance.

(3) About a kilometre along this section of riverside path (now to a lower standard [2013]) and before the Allander Water joins the River Kelvin – behind trees – we turn right onto the line of a dismantled railway (marked by telegraph poles). Soon, the narrow path bears left as it moves to join the River Kelvin. It can be slippery! The Roman Military Way bridged the Kelvin approximately 100m before the busy A879 crosses the river. Balmuildy Roman Fort was located south of the river. It seems to have been one of only two forts to have had a stone surrounding-wall (not turf) and it was erected before the turf Wall arrived.

Wall Day 2: Bearsden to Kirkintilloch

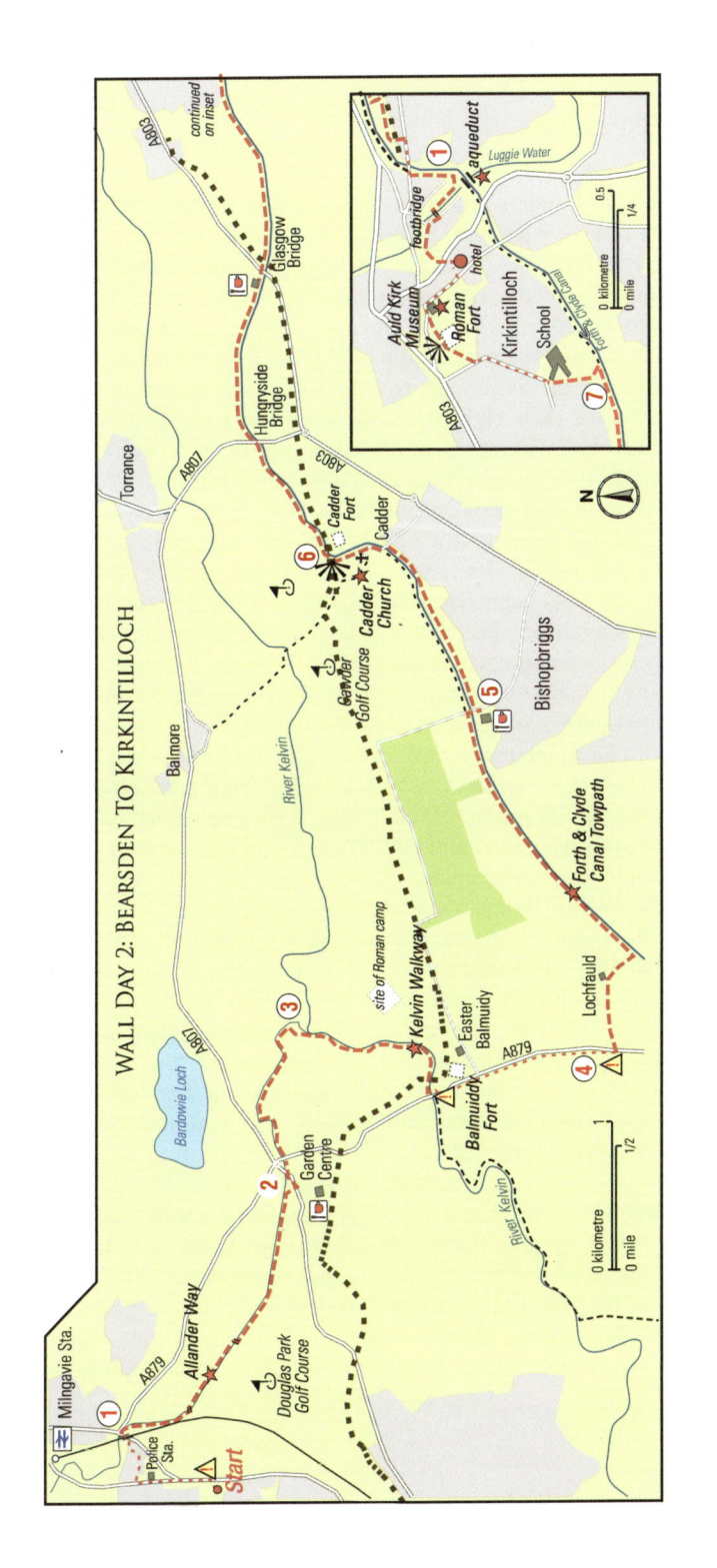

The fort builders left 'lugs' or stone-wall protuberances sticking out, to receive what they evidently expected to be a stone Antonine Wall, like Hadrian's. So, did nobody tell them the Wall would be turf, or did someone change the plans? There is evidence that this fort was destroyed twice but reoccupied twice. Little trace remains on the ground. There are (dormant?) plans for a visitor centre here.

We cross the footbridge over the River Kelvin, beside the A879, and then **we turn right up steps onto the road and cross with extreme care.** Go left, to walk southwards on the footway and view the Fort site (left). Keep ahead at a junction, towards 'Possil'. We have to walk a further 1 km up the footway of this nasty, busy, road with greenery hanging low (2012) over our way; and if it's raining, we'll get drenched with spray.

(4) We pass industrial premises called 'Luddon' (right)**,** but stay on the main road, crossing a side road on the right. Beyond a courtyard housing development (right), we take the *next left turn* – crossing with care – towards Lochfauld. Turn right in front of those premises onto a wheel track. At the end of this, *continue* down a short trodden path to turn left on the Forth and Clyde Canal towpath. (½ km before we reach the 'Leisuredrome' (below) a sign points left, north, to 'Site of former Mavis Valley' a mining village, home to 22 miners who were overcome by fumes following a pit fire in 1913.) We continue on the towpath.

(5) Where Balmuildy Road crosses the canal, its bridge is 10 km (6¼ miles) from the start of today's trail. If you're feeling peckish here, please note that the 'Leisuredrome' is sited across the canal. It has a café which "does food" (phone 0141 7773060). To get there, leave the towpath, cross the canal on Balmuildy Road Bridge, and you'll soon find the café beside the pool in the Leisuredrome, on your right. As it happens, our Antonine Trail has decided to cross the canal here, anyway, and to follow the canal on what boaters call the 'offside', the opposite side from the towpath. So, after your break, or in any event, look for the offside path and continue to follow the canal on this pleasant alternative route which soon passes through trees. We come down to the next bridge, re-cross the canal and turn right to resume our towpath trail. Ignore a road on our left which goes to *Cawder* Golf Club, so posh that the surrounding area is called *Cadder*! This name, Cadder, seems to have been widely in use. It appears on maps in various forms and at

various sites along some 10 km of the canal. We continue by the canal side. Soon, by a jetty, a short diversion (left) leads to Cadder Church. Here in the grave yard is a small stone building, complete with fireplace, where watchmen could look out for grave robbers.

Thomas Muir – you may have spotted 'Thomas Muir Trail' signs – was an Elder here. His claim to fame was his belief that church members, not the laird, should choose their minister. Thomas was arrested and tried for suggesting this and was transported to Australia! But his view prevailed and Thomas got home to Scotland. After our visit, or in any event, we continue along the towpath.

(At the beginning of this book, I mentioned the John Muir Way. On our Antonine Trail, I can imagine confusion arising between the Muir Way and the Muir Trail. Let's suppose there is a chance meeting of Way/Trail followers:

"Are you with Tom?"
"No we're with John."
Our rejoinder will be: "We're with Antonine!")

(6) *Where the canal turns ninety degrees to the right,* the course of the Antonine Wall comes in from the left by a wooded bank and crosses the canal. Old steps (left) go up to gain us a Roman viewpoint. Cadder Fort, destroyed by sand quarrying, was behind the bank we see across the right angle turn of the canal. In 1 km, we pass under Hungryside Bridge. And in a further 1 km, we arrive at The Stables restaurant and bar beside Glasgow Bridge (phone 01429 838720). About here (see map), we again cross the line of the Wall though we can see no trace whatsoever. It, and we, are heading for Kirkintilloch by slightly divergent routes. One kilometre further along the towpath, just as we see houses down on our left, we ignore a path (left) signed 'Torrance 2½ (50 mins)', but we continue on the towpath signed 'Kirkintilloch, a Walkers are Welcome Town' oh, good! Gentle curves take us past houses with moorings (right) including 'Joe's Wharf' (2013).

(7) Approximately 100 m *before* a footbridge, shaped like the prow of a ship, which spans the canal, we turn left – away from the canal – down a path taking us past a school (right) and up to a road junction. Bear right onto Bellfield Road past the entrance to St Ninian's High School and then Westermains Bowling Club. Cross

the mouth of Northbank Road (right) and curve down to the next junction where we cross the mouth of Union Street (right).

Then immediately, walk up short narrow Camphill Avenue which heads off half right. All of a sudden, we have an awful lot to take on board: First 'Kirkintilloch' is a corrupted version of 'Caerpentaloch' meaning the fort at the head of the ridge, a fair description! Secondly, Camphill Avenue is actually on the line of the Antonine Ditch with the Wall parallel on our right. Thirdly, Camphill refers to the Roman Fort or Camp on this very hill. At the top of this Avenue, turn right between trees to (try to) find two plaques on the grass explaining that in the 1950s the stone base of the Wall was uncovered here (but is, unfortunately, now covered with grass). Continuing slowly on the path through the Park, we pass a fountain commemorating Faustina, Antonine's daughter. His wife, you may recall, was also called Faustina. Next, a bandstand (right) and a raised site of a medieval motte both occupy the site of the Kirkintilloch Roman Fort. Do take in the views!

TWO TOWNS IN THE ROMAN EMPIRE!

TAKE THE PATH ADJACENT TO AULD KIRK MUSEUM

We leave the Fort site via the 'triumphal' War Memorial Gates and bear right where we see a fancy top on a gable (Old Kirk) and we walk down the narrow footpath immediately adjacent to the left side of this building. The Auld Kirk Museum has a small Roman section (open Tue to Sat). Go down the steps at the front of the Museum – noting, on the top step, a map of the Roman Empire which marks this town. Turn right on the shopping street which you can cross at a signalled crossing. If you need food for tomorrow, now is your chance. Turn left into Broadcroft, a narrow one-way street (opposite the Regent Shopping Centre). Opposite the end of the short street we find Smith's Hotel, offering food and accommodation: Address: 4 David Donnelly Place, G66 1DD; Tel: 0141 775 0398.

THAT'S THE END OF OUR SECOND 'WALL DAY'. FOUR TO GO!

WALL DAY THREE
KIRKINTILLOCH (SMITH'S HOTEL)
TO CASTLECARY (HOTEL): 16 km (10 miles)

Note:
If the weather is good, today may be a highlight of your walk. We are close to, or on, The Antonine Wall for almost all today's Trail. Some five kilometres of Forth and Clyde Canal, including two exciting underpasses underneath the canal, take us to Twechar (where there is a B&B). We then follow about 11 km along the Wall, as it crosses Barr Hill and Crow Hill, each with a Roman Fort – and between these, Castle Hill (*another* Castle Hill), site of a prehistoric fort. We encounter some of the best preserved lengths of dramatic Ditch along our entire Trail. Castlecary Hotel, at the end of today is named after tomorrow morning's Roman Fort.

A good place for lunching today, although 600m off the Trail, is the Boathouse Pub and Restaurant with Rooms at Auchinstarry Marina G65 9SG; tel. 01236 829 200. (It is on the B802 Kilsyth to Croy road.)

Let's Walk! Use the map.
Come out of the front, restaurant, door of Smith's Hotel and turn right down a path and steps to the A8006. Cross at the signalled pedestrian crossing here and then turn left and turn right down (the lower section of) Broadcroft. Before you reach a main road, below, turn right onto a footpath leading between brick blocks of flats and go along the continuing street with parking for cars at each side. At the end of this road (sign: Lion Bank), turn right at the T-junction and soon cross the footbridge on your left, signed 'Strathkelvin Railway Path (S)'. Go down the ramp on the far side of the Luggie Water and walk upstream past Campsie View Nursing Home (left). Just before the big stone arched bridge, note that our Trail will go up the steps on our left, to the canal towpath. *But first,* let's take a look at that big stone arched aqueduct. This is the 1770s Luggie Aqueduct, designed originally by John Smeaton. Three quarters of a century later, a branch line from the Edinburgh and Glasgow Railway was threaded under the aqueduct on a deck comprising a

long two-arched culvert over the river: a remarkable double decker arrangement. Now, the railway has long gone but the canal is still in business! Note how, in addition to the normal vertical arch which holds up the canal water, there is a *horizontal arch* which resists sideways pressure from the water. Lesson over: we can return to those steps up to the towpath.

(1) Turn left on the towpath and at the next (road) bridge over the canal, cross the road carefully, and then turn right to walk up the left roadside footway. Bear left, i.e. ahead, at a mini-roundabout (2013), then turn first left into 'Bank's Road', soon going right with the road. The houses on our right are *on* the Antonine Wall! The canal is below us (left). Take the paved footpath parallel to the road and, at its far end, turn left down a grassy footpath. Soon we find ourselves on another 'offside' footpath, above the canal. The Ordnance Survey map names the housing area south of the canal and south of the Antonine Wall and to our right as 'Cleddans'. We passed a Cleddans Farm on Wall Day One. Where a pipe bridge crosses the canal, the Wall came closer to the canal, soon to cross to the far side. You can mark this spot by identifying a large boulder (right) and where, also, our path drops closer to the canal.

THE LARGE BOULDER; WITH DITCH REVEALED BY RAIN PUDDLE

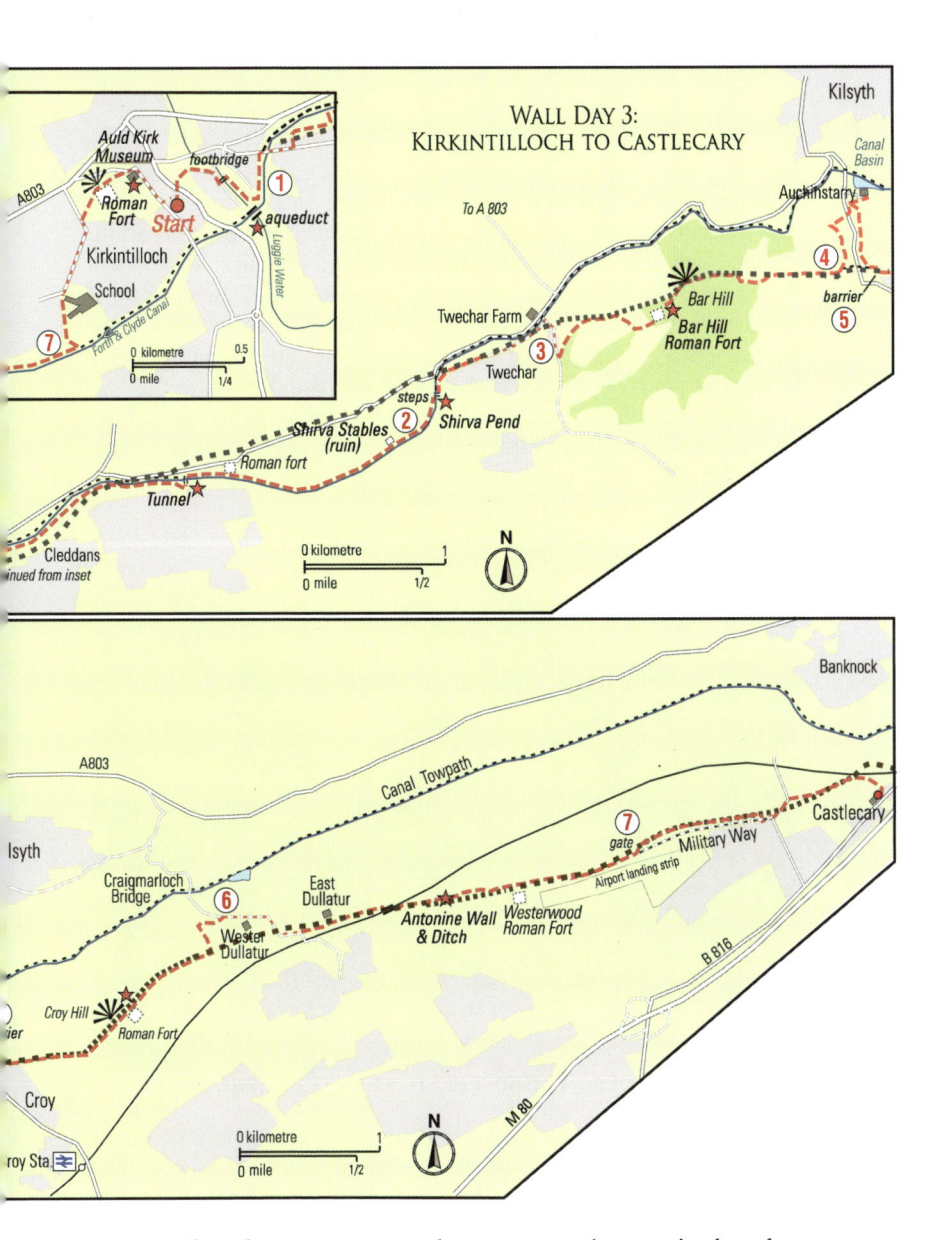

Presently, where we can see – but cannot read – a notice board on the towpath side of the canal, our Trail veers away from the water's edge. Follow it, but bear left at sign 'Tintock Wood'. Before housing, turn left to take the tunnel under the canal. The headroom sign says 4'-9" or 1.3m. It is much more along the centre-line but it defeated the Google Street-View car. At the far side *turn left* up to the towpath and that notice board, and left again on the towpath to resume our journey. Soon, a farm steading building, now modern housing (left) is on the same site as was the Roman fort of Auchendavy. Here, the B8023 road is thought to lie on the Roman Military Way which seems to have gone through the centre of the Fort. Our path offers safer walking than the road does.

About 1.3 km (¾ mile) past Auchendavy, we find on our left the safely fenced-off ruins of the rather elegant Shirva Stables (for canal horses).

PLAQUE AT SHIRVA PEND. TURN LEFT HERE!

(2) In 300m, as we round a left curve, we must not miss *Shirva Pend.* Look out for a plaque by the towpath showing how we can use the pend to cross under the canal here. DO NOT FAIL TO TURN SHARP LEFT down the forty-odd steps to the side of the burn which flows westwards under the canal through Shirva Pend. Walk through the pend. (Don't worry: there is a raised footway!) An ugly black pipe, attached to the soffit of the pend, seems to have carried Twechar sewage to a disposal plant next to old Shirva Farm.

If, as it seems, the pipe *is* disused, I hope someone thinks of removing it. *Immediately at the end of the pend,* TURN SHARP LEFT up a dark cutting which leads us onto a footpath which lies on top of, and runs along, the Antonine Wall. The Ditch runs along by our left hand side. Our path becomes a track which becomes a road and they lead us to the road which crosses the canal at Twechar Bridge. **(Twechar Farm B&B is north of the canal, here.)**

(3) Our Trail turns right, up the road and away from the canal.

THE SIGN ON THE RIGHT HAS 'BAR HILL' (Two words)

But a few metres from the canal look over a field gate, behind which the Ditch and Wall extend clearly uphill. We should continue on the road for a further 150m, till a sign 'Barhill Fort' (left) points up a track to Bar Hill Fort. (Note: Barrhill Tavern is a few yards up the road, beyond the track, tel. 01236 827121; you may find it closed). Our track joins the Wall and follows it for a while (keep to the main track) then curves right away from it. Just by woodland (right), is a tall pole (left) with a John Muir Way sign pointing left. We turn left here through a gate that looks like a kissing gate onto a broad, straight, grassy, path leading to the south-west corner of the tidily presented Bar Hill Roman Fort.

THE SIGN ACROSS THE ROAD HAS 'BARRHILL TERRACE' (Two Rs)

I have merely copied 'Bar Hill', 'Barhill', and 'Barrhill' as I found them – I tend to think 'Bar Hill' may be the correct spelling. 'Bar' Farm is on our way up the hill (per Ordnance Survey map), though a sign says 'Barr Farm'. There *should be a double 'r'* according to a local landowner who, when I enquired why Historic Scotland used only *one 'r'*, explained: *"They're English!"*

If, on entry to the fort, we manage to turn ourselves to the left through about 20 degrees and amble up the grass, we should come up to where the outline of the headquarters building is marked out on the ground in concrete. In its courtyard we find the fort's well – more or less on the top of the rise. The bathhouse is downhill, in the north-west corner. This fort is, somewhat exceptionally; *separate* from the Antonine Wall by some 30 or 40 metres. In fact, the military way passed between them. This is the highest (150 m) fort on the Wall. Check out the views. This is another location where a fort by Agricola seems to have predated the Antonine effort.

BAR HILL BATHS

(Just for the record: The Romans' Military Way can be followed eastwards from the mid point of the east side of the fort; but you would miss the dramatic Ditch, ahead.)

Leave Bar Hill Fort diagonally opposite your entry point, via the northeast corner, into a loose grouping of sycamore trees, and birch, where you should spot the Antonine Ditch to the left of Castle Hill. Go down then up to face this smallish, but steep, hill where a prehistoric fort was located. On your way up, you can pause to read an interpretation panel. Continue over this lump, sorry hill, past a trig. point, then down to follow the Antonine Wall and Ditch. This stretch of Ditch – for over ½ km – is quite spectacular and dramatic. And it is steep: don't slip! We come down to a cross dyke (and an Antonine Wall sign) where we must turn right and go down to a path or track where we turn left and slowly are restored to the line of the ditch. Because the gradient is easier, the ditch has been fairly – or unfairly – flattened and our straight track follows its line down to the B802 (Kilsyth to Croy) road.

(4) **BE ALERT!** 200m before you reach the B802 road, you'll see a pedestrian gate on your left with signs Auchinstarry and Public

Footpath to Auchinstarry Basin. If you want a civilised lunch stop at The Boathouse (tel. 01236 829 200) turn left through the gate – a fingerpost sign says Auchinstarry and Canal ½ mile. <u>Directions</u>: Follow the main path, down then up a little, then bearing right to a gate onto the road. Cross and walk left down the roadside footway. You can soon access some paths in front of The Boathouse *before* reaching a traffic roundabout. After your break: To go uphill *without crossing the road*, go into the Sense and Sensibilities Garden; make for a white-tiled totem pole and take the uphill path, soon passing a Nethercroy sign. After a bench, an unofficial path bears left (ahead) and is slightly shorter. On rejoining the official path, follow Castlecary sign. Turn right at a wide surfaced area (sign: Castlecary 4½ miles). The **barrier gate** ahead is referred to in the next paragraph.

If you decide not to visit Auchinstarry, then directly across the road from our track is a kissing gate on the line of the Wall. Cross carefully and go through the gate. *Two* paths start here. It is a fraction shorter to choose the *right fork*. (They both head for Castlecary and they soon join up.) At a sort of road, ahead, go through a kissing gate and turn right. Within moments, by a **barrier gate**, turn left to start uphill by a sign: 'The Antonine Walkway Craigmarloch via Croy Hill'.

> (At this point, those wishing to catch a train can go ahead – instead of left – to join the public road, where they bear left to reach Croy Station in 1 km. It is preferable to walk along the right-hand footway which soon allows one to utilise the slightly shorter old road).

(5) We are now heading towards Croy Hill, with a spectacular view of the ascent path. We keep going ahead when the road curves right; and we soon find we are walking *in* the Antonine Ditch. Go through a kissing gate, labelled 'Croy Hill'. As we head uphill it is worth detouring left once or twice to inspect the Ditch, since our path, though parallel, is now set a few metres back. In fact there is soon a cliff, just north of the line of the Wall. You may spot that those do-things-by-the-book Romans actually dug a length of their ditch *at the foot of the cliff.* Take care not to fall over the edge of the Empire!

CROY HILL DESCENT WITH THE STEEP RISE (centre)

We go *over* the summit and start to descend, wondering where Croy Hill Roman Fort actually is. Answer: on the way down. But first, we find ourselves in a sort of dip with at least three trodden ways ahead. I think most folk masochistically choose the left hand way which soon rises most steeply! We can go this way, too, where we have the reassurance of the Ditch to our left. Croy Hill Roman Fort is found on the next bit of descent. It is about half the area of Bar Hill Fort and is not only less well-presented; it probably isn't presented at all. In fact, you may be hard pressed to identify it. There are some – *relatively modern* – bits of walls of a farm and the odd tree or two. Nevertheless, on a couple of visits, the groups I've been with have chosen this spot for a picnic.

When we decide to continue with our Trail, follow the Antonine Ditch. WARNING: Ignore another, well-used, path which crosses the line of the Ditch but heads the wrong way – a bit east of north. In about ½ km of descent, following the Ditch, we come to a cross path on the line of an old mineral railway. Turn left (sign: Castlecary 3¼ miles). Very soon we turn right (sign: Castlecary 3 miles), down through a gate on a path/track which passes a small car park and comes down to a public road which has come uphill from Craigmarloch Bridge over the canal.

(6) We turn right uphill along the road, soon passing Wester Dullatur Farm (right). The road bends right then, as it crosses the line of the Wall, it bends left. For a further three miles we are effectively 'walking the Wall' and have a good opportunity to study the effects of the years upon it. At a junction, *we ignore a right turn* – where some road signs are a bit confusing, and where the 'main' road passes under the railway line – but *we carry* **straight** *on* past some cottages and East Dullatur (left). Presently the Wall and our route both cross under the railway. Beyond, i.e. south of, the railway, our route becomes a track – muddy in places – but rises uphill with one of the *deepest and most spectacular sections* of the Antonine Ditch over a fence (right). I suggest this part of the Trail may not pull in the crowds: but it *should!* Presently, we are aware of a golf course on each side of the Trail. Then we pass the north side of the former Westerwood Farm which is fitted into the north east corner of Westerwood Roman Fort. (On a sunny day, it is worth popping in here for a nosey look around and to check the bounds of the Fort.) Otherwise, **and I stress this:** OUR TRAIL DOES <u>NOT</u> TURN RIGHT AT WESTERWOOD; it goes *ahead* on a grassy, less trodden route but official gates soon give us confidence. A couple of hundred metres along the left edge of an open area, our Trail – <u>almost unexpectedly</u> – curves sharply right, goes through a gate, and curves back left. We are rather close to the north boundary fence of Wardpark Air Landing Strip. For the next half kilometre navigation is rather tricky. Until more people make this way more trodden, we have to soldier on through, seeking glimpses of reassuring marker discs (some of which are sensibly located) and passing – perhaps between – two buildings, the remains of the hamlet of Arniebog.

(7) We come to a point where the track we have been struggling to follow, curves left to cross the line of the Antonine Wall. From this point, the Ditch is accompanied on its way by a belt of trees which starts here. You will be tempted to go up to it by a signpost about the Antonine Wall which is sited at the start of the wood by an inviting gate. This is, indeed, our official Antonine Trail.

NOW STOP: READ AHEAD!

Note: If the weather has recently been fine and dry, then you may indeed go up to that tempting signpost and make your way along the belt of trees by way of a series of large-capacity metal kissing-gates. (But: cattle seem to find these gates attractive and, in wet weather, they enjoy pounding their feet up and down in the mud, and it may take you an hour to advance one kilometre. In that event, you can follow the Military Way. This takes us AHEAD on a lovely grassy track: an inviting, easy stroll located parallel to the wooded Antonine Ditch but located some 20 to 50 metres to the south of it.)

In either event, we emerge on a road. Bear left on it, but soon right again up into a field. Keep to the left edge and follow the Antonine Wall (left) till we are obliged by a railway line, which cuts across the wall, to curve gently right, still following the field edge until we are channelled into the rear car park of Castlecary Hotel via its special 'Roman Soldiers' gate. Reception, and the end of this section are round the front, (Tel: 01324 840233; postcode is G68 0HD).

END OF THIRD 'WALL DAY'. THREE TO GO!

HOW TO CELEBRATE VICTORY

Note:
The half-way point in *your* Antonine Trail depends upon which 'extra' bits you have decided to include. The chances are *your* half-way point may arrive during Wall Day Four, near to Falkirk. So I am giving you this extra bit of reading before Wall Day Four.

We first need to bring together some thoughts about space and time.

Space:
The Romans had an important portal for crossing their Antonine Wall at their fortlet at Watling Lodge – about a kilometre east of the Falkirk Wheel. They did not require a bigger fort here, because they *already had one* at Camelon, one kilometre *north* of the Wall. Camelon Fort predated the Wall and remained in use while the Wall was manned – part of the evidence for supposing the Romans felt secure and safe even on the 'wrong' side of their frontier.

Our M80 and M9 motorways meet at a point on the map like an arrow pointing north. The Roman road going north from Camelon ran up and now bisects the angle between these motorways. Well, we all have to find a northbound way across the River Forth!

Time:
PART ONE referred to *two* events in 142 AD. First, Roman coins of this date commemorated a victory – presumably over the south of Scotland. Secondly, Roman construction squads started building the Antonine Wall. It seems to me the Romans were saying: "OK! You are defeated. Just stay there and behave yourselves."

Victory: Part of the Commemoration:
At various places along the Antonine Wall, we find evidence that Roman soldiers felt a continuing security in *remembering their victory* by actually worshipping the goddess of Victory. What is the evidence?

I rather imagine that skilled Roman stone-masons and stone-carvers who, during the previous twenty years had worked on

Hadrian's Wall, and who then, with their colleagues, marched north to form the new Antonine Wall construction gangs – only to find that a *turf* rampart was on the agenda. For whatever reason (pride, or the employment of masons), the Antonine Wall was liberally provided with 'distance slabs' of stone, sometimes elaborately carved. The slabs proclaimed each length of Wall that whomsoever had just completed. At least four of these (found so far) – one found in 1969 – feature the goddess Victory. In one, she raises a laurel wreath to the beak of an eagle – the bird which features so strongly in Roman insignia.

A Roman Fort Port:
The River Carron passes within a kilometre to the north of Camelon Fort. Since sea level was a bit higher in Roman times, Romans could get vessels up to Camelon at high tide. It was a Port Fort! Camelon was an important place. And it got an important shrine.

A Roman Temple to Victory:
For fifteen hundred years, from Roman times, a stone-built domed edifice stood on the north side of the River Carron not far from Camelon Fort. The building stood on a circular stone foundation. It comprised a 9m diameter cylinder, 4m tall, with metre thick walls, surmounted by a 9m diameter hemisphere. So, its total height was about 4+4.5=8.5m. Sketches show a circular hole in the top, like the Pantheon in Rome, though this *could be* damage.

The building had carvings above its door and inside, featuring the Roman eagle and perhaps the goddess Victory. Bits of a metal statue, including a finger, were found inside; reckoned, perhaps, to have been from the goddess Victory. If this rather tenacious theory is correct, it must have helped our Romans feel more secure.

I have some bad news and some good news.

Bad News:
This structure was reckoned to be the best preserved Roman building in Britain when, in 1743, the landowner demolished it to use the stones to construct a mill dam – something to do with the Carron Iron Works. Not only is there no trace of the temple; there is no trace of the dam. It was washed away within five years. Damn!

Good News:
Before the demolition, antiquarians managed to draw very detailed plans and sketches. The proprietor of the Penicuik estate, south of Edinburgh, was so incensed at the wanton destruction that he built a full-scale replica of the temple in his grounds – which we can see to this day. Mind you, perhaps to keep it out of harm's way, he chose to erect it on the roof of the entrance to his stables, as a dovecote. We can surely regard this act of preservation as a Victory.

DOME ON TOP OF PENICUIK HOUSE STABLES

What's in a Name?
For centuries, locals called the Roman Dome "Arthur's Oven" because it looked like a gigantic bread oven. No one knows who Arthur may have been: King Arthur?

The pronunciation of 'Penicuik' is easy: "Penny-cook".

But the pronunciation of 'Camelon' seems surprisingly problematical. I had always given it three syllables, forming a pronunciation group with two other words: 'Camelot' of King Arthur and 'Cameron' my own first name. Seeking arbitration, I walked into a small local supermarket and asked the check-out girl: "How do you pronounce the name of this place?"

Her astonishing reply came back, "Spar"!

As far as I can ascertain, locals use two syllables sounding like "Camm-linn".

To be fair: our Romans called the place something completely different, quite lost in the mists of time. So; even the locals are in the dark about that name.

A CLOSE-UP OP THE REPLICA TEMPLE AT PENICUIK

REMEMBER: THERE ARE THREE WALL DAYS REMAINING!

WALL DAY FOUR
CASTLECARY (HOTEL)
TO FALKIRK (CENTRAL PREMIER INN): 14.5 km (9 miles)

Important note:
It is perfectly possible to combine Wall Day Four's stroll with Wall Day Five's stroll and aim directly for Beancross (Hotels) with a combined distance of about 27 km (16 miles).

Our logistical difficulty is that these two days include five 'side visits' which we shall certainly find to be time-consuming but which are important sight-seeing elements of this holiday walking Trail. You could make a combined single day possible if you omitted the five 'side visits'. Helpfully, this would reduce the combined distance, all the way to Beancross (Hotels), to 20 km (12 miles). Let me describe the Trail for Wall Days Four and Five – and the 'side visits' – then you can decide whether you are voting for the sight-seeing stroll or the mad dash to the finish.

Note:
For about four kilometres this morning, our canal and our Wall are closely, sometimes too closely, associated. But today and tomorrow are our real side visit, holidaymaker-mode days. We have two more canal underpasses to visit and in side visit number three, our visit to the amazing Falkirk Wheel; we may get the chance of a boat trip up and down the wheel in which – to get to the turning area at the top – we are taken by boat through the tunnel which ingenious modern civil engineers cut *underneath* The Antonine Wall. So, we were excited about walking under the canal? Now we can sail on the canal under The Wall!

Let me emphasise my warning about sight-seeing time. Many families plan an entire day around the Falkirk Wheel – and they come by car – we shall very likely use the café facilities and have the boat trip – and we're on foot. AND by the time we arrive here we've already done two side visits and we have wandered happily around the Rough Castle Fort site, which is on the Trail line. Got the picture? We have to decide whether we are mad-dash hikers or Roman Relic explorers.

Let's walk! Use the map.
Leave Castlecary Hotel by turning left to go under the high arches, noting an old bridge, left, crossing the river. Keep off the M80 motorway. Swing right on B816 road to cross the motorway. Then:

> Side visit number one. To find Castlecary Roman Fort, turn first right (sign 'Walton'), then turn left into a cul-de-sac. Soon we find two signs (right) about Castlecary Roman Fort. As you will discover, it is possible to enter the field here, through a gate. This was the other stone-built fort on the Antonine Wall. Go forward to a group of trees, passing a few stones of the east boundary wall, and you will come to foundations of the headquarters complex. The site seems hemmed-in but it has, after all, been rather trashed by people aiming roads and railways at it. Return to the B816 and turn right.

(1) Next, a little past the M80 exit, turn left on the signed footpath cycle-way to go down to the old road bridge over the Forth and Clyde Canal. Cross the bridge and go eastwards on the towpath. In 1.5 km (a mile), at the third canal lock, we find Underwood Lockhouse (tel: 01324 849111, or 849227) with a car park across the canal (and a footbridge leading to it). This establishment, according to its sign, serves 'Food all Day' but, seemingly "does not open till about 5 pm" I was told. *However, it was severely fire-damaged in 2013.*

The Antonine Wall has been getting closer to the canal and, by the Lockhouse, seems to have been eaten up by the canal excavations – another way to trash a monument. In less than a kilometre, we become aware of Seabegs Wood across the canal. The Wall has by now climbed up from the canal and is carefully protected at Seabegs.

THE MILITARY WAY IN SEABEGS WOOD – LOOKING WEST

Side visit number two. We can get to Seabegs by another pedestrian underpass below the canal. Again, it's a water culvert with a raised footpath. There's a ramp down to this from the towpath, but it's easy to miss because it's further along than you expect, so you'll miss it if you're chatting.

WALL DAY 4: CASTLECARY TO FALKIRK

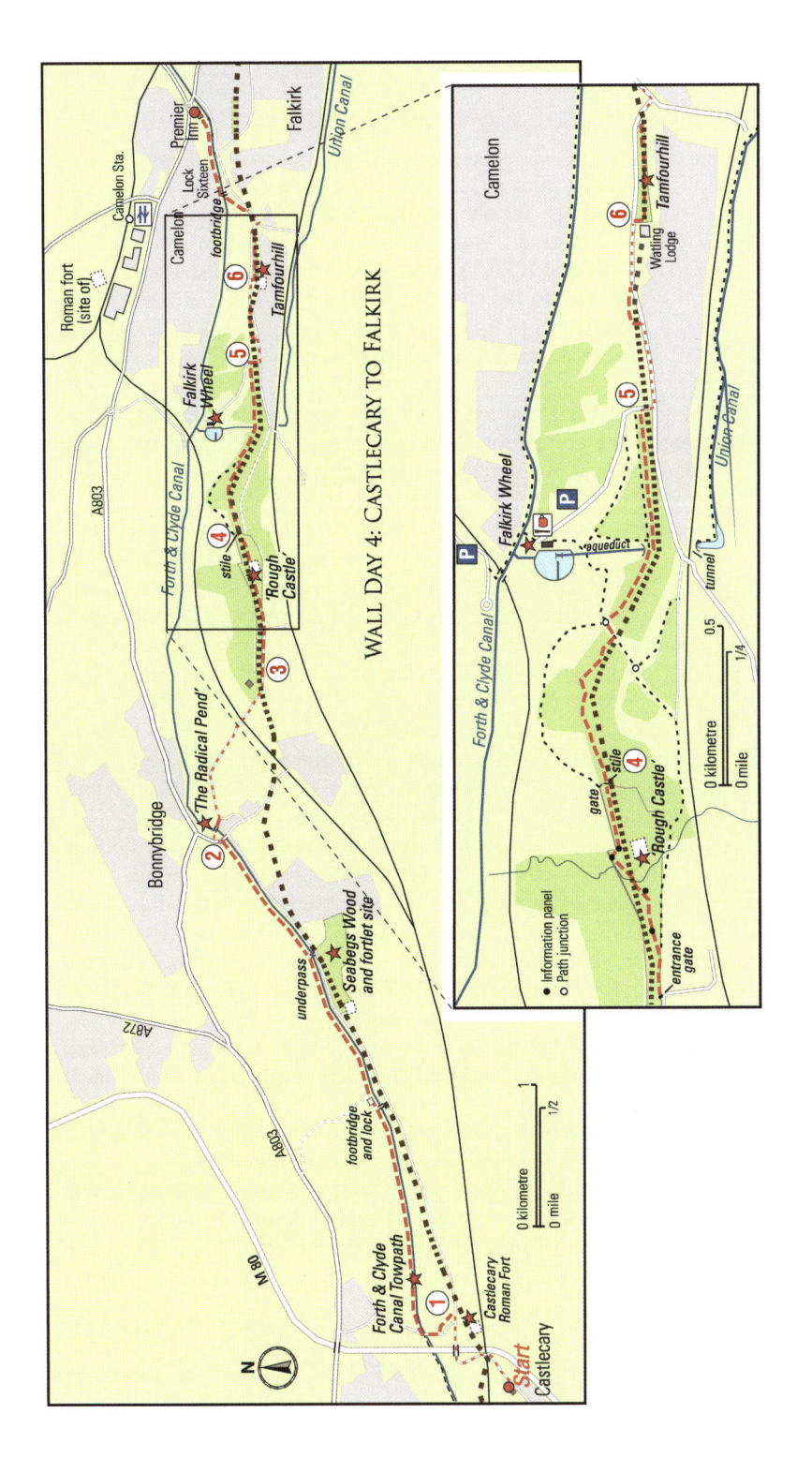

I have allowed 1.5 km (1 mile) for our visit – so go! Warning: the subway path is on a raised line in the centre of this pend. Watch your step in the gloom and it can be VERY SLIPPERY especially at the south end. Go through the gate to the site, find the military way and use it to go westwards to the top of the site but choose a different way back down to the canal underpass.

1 km further along the canal, we come to a lifting road bridge. Although we are at Bonnybridge and even if you think the lifting bridge is bonny, we should note that the river that has been tracking the route of the canal, but down in the valley on our left, is named the Bonny Water. So Bonnybridge, the *bridge,* takes the A803 across this wee river. Well, I'm glad we cleared that up.

(2) We leave the canal at the lifting bridge. Here's how: go up from the towpath to the road, cross carefully and turn left, downhill. As soon as you can, go down to the *right* – off the road – passing the Auto Doctor Garage (2013) to 'The Radical Pend' canal creep. This is *another underpass* below the canal. Here the bed of the stream serves as a sett-paved narrow road. Again we have a raised footway, but with a handrail. Go through and up the other side. Bear left as you emerge from the gloom – gently uphill. The road serves development which is an odd mixture of housing and industry.

About a kilometre from the canal our Trail takes us over a bridge over the railway. We pass the gates of Bonnyside House (left).

(3) Ahead of us the track curves left; but just before this curve, we cross the Antonine Ditch and Wall. The Ditch is very obvious over the masonry wall on our left. *Then look to the right* to discern the clear trace of the Wall and the Ditch coming across the field. On we go, past the rather overgrown garden (left) with a pedestrian gate padlocked from the *outside,* – are we trying to keep them *in?* Next, we come to Historic Scotland's Rough Castle site: not a huge Roman Fort, but one of interest. Go in the first pedestrian entrance where a notice, at a good viewpoint to look along the Ditch and Wall, tells us that the fort 'lies 300 yards to the east'.

The *main entrance* to the site is 300 yards ahead, and the Roman Fort is about 800 yards (nearly half a mile) beyond the notice.

I suggest we continue walking along the vehicle track from that pedestrian entrance, because we can see into the site well enough *and* we are reckoned to be on the Roman Military Way which, you recall, ran the entire length of the Wall. In 300 yards we come to the main entrance to the site – no sign of a fort.

At the time of writing, Historic Scotland seems to be renewing signs. The (temporary) sign on the main gate reads 'Help keep Historic Scotland free from dog fouling'! Falkirk Council has helpfully posted a more graphic sign on the same subject on the gate. Go in the gate – we're still on the military way. Go up to read a (first) information panel, past a vehicle turning area. The panel majors on a *prehistoric settlement,* but includes a locator plan showing the Roman Fort, ahead.

Our trail takes us straight over the grass to an open group of trees to find a second information panel. This second panel explains the Wall construction. Turn round to overlook the fort. Our way now bears left to enter the ditch and to go down to cross a footbridge over the burn. (Note: we shall then bear right – up into the fort itself, before heading left to cross a Roman ramp over the Antonine Ditch to the last two information panels.)

WESTERN RAMPARTS OF ROUGHCASTLE – LOOKING SOUTH

The Rough Castle Roman Fort, once you're up, can be viewed from various vantage points. You will have noticed the various defensive ditches as you climbed up to the top.

Now go north to cross the Roman ramp over the Antonine Ditch. This was the Romans' main 'north door' to this part of Pictland and, to your left, the third information panel describes the *Lilia* which you will want to examine (and imagine getting trapped in!) Now go over to the nearby fourth panel – just beyond the ramp over the ditch. This gives a good overview, and the Ditch looks great from here. Our Trail heads east, following now the north side of the Antonine Ditch. You should be aware of the Fort annexe in the woodland across the ditch (right).

Our trodden Trail goes over the stile into woodland ahead, outside Historic Scotland's site.

> (*Note:* Our trail can be both muddy and slippery after heavy rain. There is an easier, but slightly longer route, signposted down to the left of the stile. It is slightly further because it heads downhill – towards the railway – and back up again. If you *must* go that way, head for the path leading *up and over the top of the Falkirk Wheel Site.* A sign will say 'Tamfourhill'.)

(4) Over the stile, our trodden Trail follows the Ditch (right) as we slowly begin to lose height. When we come to a direction sign, ignore it completely – apart from making sure we *go straight on* – in an unsigned direction. Then, AT A FORK AHEAD, TAKE THE LEFT BRANCH OF THREE. Follow this trodden way, and presently becoming aware of a good section of the Antonine Ditch on our right. (For information: the central branch of the three follows the south side if the ditch.)

Eventually we arrive at a good cross path, forming an obstruction over the Ditch. This was a mine railway. Turn left here to a path junction, **with the Falkirk Wheel Aqueduct ahead and a short-cut to side visit number three.** Otherwise, turn right here to 'Tamfourhill' – at the point where the people from the 'easier route' rejoin the Trail. This takes us to a bench (right) overlooking the Falkirk Wheel and its approach aqueduct. This modern section of canal construction drove a tunnel under the Antonine Wall. I think we've decided that trashing of the monument has had to stop!

Side visit number three. If you want to spend time at this unique civil engineering feature and major tourist attraction, go down the path starting beyond the safety fence and then proceed down the far – east – side of the aqueduct to get to the visitor centre and café. They organise boat trips up the wheel, through the tunnel, and back down again. Or, you can yourself walk through the tunnel and under the Antonine Wall, have a look around, and come back again. Allow at least two hours: one for the boat trip; one for waiting and eating. (Tel 01324 619888).

Otherwise, *look to your right just as you come to the place where the Trail crosses the aqueduct: just past that bench (right) a small footbridge crosses the path-side ditch (also right), and you can scramble up* to the edge of the Antonine Ditch where you can turn left for a good study of the Ditch as we walk along. For our purposes, this unofficial path is our Trail and is preferable to the parallel official path which we have risen above. **This section of the Ditch is quite dramatic and you can see the flattish area – the 'berm' – on the far side, with obvious remnants of the Antonine Wall itself beyond that.**

(5) When you reach a road (the access to the Falkirk Wheel Site), cross and turn right. Almost at once, at a mini-roundabout, turn left along the roadside footway. (We are on Tamfourhill Road.) Just past a house with a drive and stone gate posts, we can go left (sign 'Antonine Wall') to look at the Ditch. A plaque here has vanished (2014). We have to return to the roadside footway by the way we left it, because it is *not* a through path. We pass another house (left), (nos. 22 & 20). DO NOT try to go left into the overgrown woodland, until we are DIRECTLY OPPOSITE Cumbrae Drive (on the right). Here we turn left on a narrow path (covered in rubbish in 2014) which leads down into the Antonine Ditch and up the other side, where we turn right to join a rough path which skirts along the north side of the Ditch, through woodland. Stay on the path till it brings us back onto the road. Cross the road and turn left.

Just past a house, is a Historic Scotland plaque about 'Antonine Wall Watling Lodge East'. Go through the gap into this site, where you can see a picture. Walk along the site to come back to the road by a gate at the far end. This takes you past the house here which blocks the ditch. In some ways, the construction of this villa 'Watling Lodge' was unfortunate. It is just at the point where a Roman fortlet guarded the main route from the south where it crossed to the north side of the Wall and the important fort at Camelon about 1 km to the north. About half the length of the original connecting road is still in use! Of course, from the point of view of the Watling Lodge builder, the Roman facilities here formed the perfect base for a house site.

(6) Immediately east of Watling Lodge, enter the gate on your right and go up the steps to find the so-called best preserved section of Ditch along the entire Antonine Wall. Walk – you choose the route – along to the far (east) end of this Tamfourhill site, and go through the gate to continue to the end of Tamfourhill Road. At a T-junction, turn left (it's Glenfuir Road) towards the Forth and Clyde Canal.*

* If you are combining Wall Days Four and Five, omit Side visit number four and, from the road junction east of the Tamfourhill site, turn right here and head up under the rail bridge (see tomorrow).

If you bear left on a footpath, this takes you more quickly to the canal side where you go right, soon to cross the canal at a road bridge. Turn right on the far side, crossing the road with care, to walk down the broad towpath, passing a pub and canal locks. Keep your eyes peeled for the canal-side gate giving access on your left to the end of today's Falkirk Premier Inn and Beefeater Restaurant.

THAT'S THE END OF OUR FOURTH 'WALL DAY'. TWO TO GO!

WALL DAY FIVE
FALKIRK (CENTRAL PREMIER INN)
TO BEANCROSS (HOTELS): 12 km (7½ miles)

Note:
This day offers us a short walk with two side visits which you can omit if combining today with yesterday. After a visit to the Bantaskine stretch of Ditch and Wall, we make our way to the Union (narrow) Canal, because I could not resist taking you through the Falkirk Tunnel! After 4.5 km (2¾ miles) of towpath, including the tunnel, we go over Callendar Woods Hill to the delights of Callendar Park. After a side visit to Callendar House, we rejoin The Antonine Wall on an excellent stretch which passes the House, continuing along a road built *on* the Ditch uphill, then down, to Beancross.

Callendar House has a tearoom and we do pass a fish restaurant (see text).

Let's walk! Use the map.
Come out of the Premier Inn via the gate to the canal towpath.

> Side visit number four. Cross the canal at a nearby lock. (Top gates are better: bottom ones sometimes swing open.) Cross the road in front of you and head for the side road labelled 'Anson Avenue' (which has a spacious grass area on the left of its mouth). Anson Avenue curves left then round to the right, then goes straighter, uphill. Half way round the next curve to the left, go in the gate on your left to explore 250 metres of Ditch and Wall. Return to the gate; cross Anson Avenue; and take the grassy path in front of you which goes down the Ditch. On reaching the road below – watching your footing – turn right; (this is Westburn Avenue). Turn left on the main road, (Glenfuir Road) and walk up it, ignoring all junctions, to pass under a red-brick-supported rail bridge, mentioned in the footnote towards the end of yesterday.

(1) Once through the bridge, turn left and up a track to the Union Canal towpath. Continue eastwards. In 1.5 km (1 mile) the towpath curves right at a grassy area before entering a cutting and a tunnel.

> (Rail travellers can get access to Falkirk High Railway Station by turning left on a path. If you need to get a travel ticket at the booking office, you can take the subway under the railway, and then go up the steps to your right and cross the car park.) (Rail travellers *arriving* at Falkirk High to start back on the Trail can, from the main station building walk to the far end of the car park, bearing right to reach the far corner, furthest from the station, where you find a secret pedestrian exit. Go down the steps to 'Drossie Road' – and another car park. Turn sharp left where there is a sign 'Path to Union Canal'. Go through the subway and, leaving the railway, continue to the canal towpath where you turn left.)

Before entering the canal tunnel which is 0.8 km (½ mile) long, you should know that the towpath does have a handrail, but there is *only* (2014) a top rail; which may pose a problem if you have a child or a dog with you. Also, water does tend to enter the tunnel from overhead. You can try turning round to judge if you're past the half way point. Beyond the tunnel, the first bridge over the canal has a cartouche bearing '1821' and with a carved rather sad head below it. On the far side of the bridge a second face is *smiling* down on us. We continue under a second bridge no. '60' and a third no. '59' when the view opens out to our left. We shall, of course, be crossing over the hill on the left horizon: but stay on the canal just now.

(2) Go under the next bridge which is no. '58' and you will soon focus your attention on the bridge beyond it, no. '57' which has distinctive iron railing parapets. Ignore 'The Old Drove Road', just go *under* the bridge and – about 100 m further on – turn left down a path by a gully and through a culvert under the railway. On the far side, we soon follow it downhill, cross a bridge, and walk up to a road noticing how you get an avenue of trees if you stop cutting your hedges. Turn right at the road and walk up the footway (not the off-road path) for a minute and a half. Look for a sign pointing left and cross the road *with great care at the brow of the hill,* where drivers can see us, towards 'Callendar Wood Path Network'. On the track, do not go to Woodend Farm but fork right at a John Muir

Way sign and enter the wood between gate posts in the high surrounding wall.

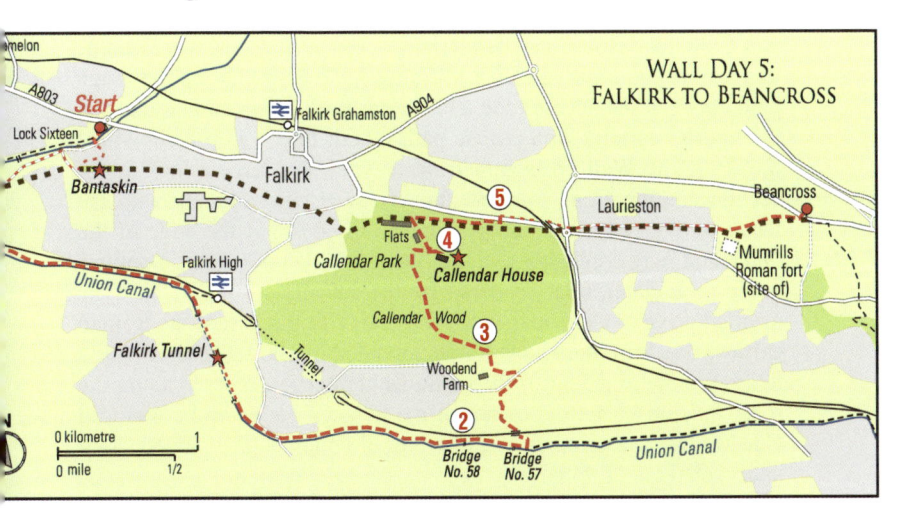

WALL DAY 5: FALKIRK TO BEANCROSS

(3) In the wood, bear left on the John Muir Way and, at a sort of track cross-roads, bearing right effectively follows the *main* track in front of you, leading gently downhill and soon curving gently right. Cross a more minor path and at the *next* junction go ahead – effectively bearing right to go more steeply downhill. At other junctions, keep ahead and DO NOT turn right where the John Muir Way turns! (You'll spot a block of flats ahead in the distance and you may see Callendar House slightly to your right.) As the trees thin out, you pass a golf area (left). At the foot, where there are toilets and a kiosk, go right.

> Side visit number five. Continue along to visit Callendar House, open to the public, free of charge (last admission 4 p.m.). There is an Antonine Wall Gallery: Go in the main door then one floor up and turn left. The 10 minute DVD will show you some of the stuff you've already seen. Also on this floor and opposite the main door is a teashop which follows the Scottish teashop tradition of closing at tea-time, but I do recommend this place.

(4) On leaving Callendar House, retrace your steps past the frontage then bear right (keeping a tree on a small tump to your right), still bearing right north-westwards to pass old stables (left) and Callendar House car park (right). (Note that you would come this way if you omitted a visit to Callendar House.) Go up the rough path between the access road and the car park. Go straight ahead at the top to continue on a tarmac path by tall flats. Stop here, where the Antonine Wall crosses in front of you. Do have a look at the section coming from your left, but we *turn right* to walk with the Ditch on our left. We are walking on the berm at the edge of the Ditch and may note a trace of the actual Wall on our right. Soon we come to an interpretation panel (right) actually *on* the Wall. The original drive to Callendar House has carved right across the Roman earthworks, forming a huge notch, intended to allow Queen Victoria to admire the grandeur of the house as her carriage passed along the road, outside. I bet the owner of the house wept when he was told Her Majesty was gazing in the wrong direction as she passed. (An apocryphal tale, I think.)

We go down leftwards to cross the drive beside a gate barrier. We go up the gentle grass ramp to take us parallel to the main road, but within the Ditch. (If the one-time owner of Callendar House had not objected to the canal-builders' *original* plan of passing their canal across Callendar Hill – to the south of the house – with boats in view, our walk would have been shorter but with no tunnel to go through.) Continue on our grassy path till, at a fence across the Wall, you may spot a Historic Scotland's, or its predecessor's, sign which not many folk seem to read. We make our way diagonally down to the lower grass area nearer the road. Continue with the Wall (right) and the road (left). Beyond the far end of that fence, the Wall is much less dramatic (trust me), so stay on the lower grass area.

(5) Cross the busy road at signalled crossing before a bus shelter. Turn right on the far side, soon to walk under a railway bridge and, presently, passing (or entering) 'benny t's fish and chips' restaurant and take-away.

Our path leads us through a subway and, at the far side, we bear *left slightly* up past houses. (DO NOT TAKE THE FOOTPATH WHICH BEARS SLIGHTLY RIGHT.) At a junction, we find we are coming up Grahamsdyke Street. Go over the cross street

(Kennetwall Drive/George Street) and continue as straight as possible. We are following a road laid originally in the Ditch. Go over another cross street, with a slight left-right zig-zag, into the continuation of Grahamsdyke Street: still on the line of the Wall. Our medieval forebears thought that local hero, Gryme, destroyed much of the Wall: 'Grymisdyke' or later 'Grahamsdyke' – whence the name of the street: either that, or Gryme Dyke meant Strong Wall.

Up ahead, where we see big trees, we move on – *still going as straight as possible* – into countryside. The old road ahead – our Trail – is closed to vehicles, so we go through the pedestrian/cycle gate. Here we are at the site of Mumrills Roman Fort (right), at 6½ acres the largest on the Wall and seemingly slightly predating the Wall building. No visible trace remains! Even earlier, Agricola seems to have built a fort just to the west, now under houses. 0.8 km (½ mile) takes us to Beancross. Once upon a time, Beancross was a village. It seems now to be a complex of hotels, dining establishment and a children's nursery. At the foot of the hill, *bear right* then, at the entrance to a pedestrian subway (on you left), you have a choice:

Either: Go through the subway, then left to find a Travelodge Hotel, West Beancross Farm, FK2 0XS, tel: 0871 984 6359; also a Metro Inn, FK2 0XS, tel: 01324 719966. There is the Beancross Family Restaurant, tel: 01324 718 333; and Chianti Restaurant, tel: 01324 715 500.

Or: Go straight on, ignoring the subway and cross the side road (on right) *with care*. In 100m you pass a bus stop then, down some steps on your right, you find a Premier Inn (Falkirk East) at Cadgers Brae, FK2 0YS, tel: 0871 527 8392, with adjoining Brewers Fayre Restaurant, tel: 0870 197 7098.

THAT'S THE END OF OUR FIFTH 'WALL DAY'. ONE TO GO!

WALL DAY SIX
BEANCROSS (HOTELS)
TO CARRIDEN HOUSE (B&B) AND ROMAN FORT: 16 km (10 miles)
OR TO THE END OF THE WALL, HARBOUR ROAD: 14 km (8½ miles)
ALTERNATIVELY TO RICHMOND PARK HOTEL: 10.5 km (6½ miles)

Today's ending options:
(1) If you are doing the Wall Days Only, the logical finishing point is at the end of the Wall in Harbour Road. Here you will find buses to Bo'ness bus station for a bus to Linlithgow, to catch yet another bus or a main line (Edinburgh-Glasgow) train. Some of you could be in you own beds at home, tonight!
(2) If you are doing the Full Walk, including the Extra Day – Beyond the Wall – you will want to consider Carriden House because you'll be at the Roman Fort site of Velunia! Carriden House offers bed and breakfast and, if you make use of it – checking prices before booking – remember that you will have to dine in Bo'ness before arrival. At the time of writing, the B&B owner is considering selling up. So: double check! Carriden was the eastmost Roman fort of the Antonine Wall. (Tomorrow's distance is calculated from Carriden.)
(3) Richmond Park Hotel may attract your attention. It's on your entry to Bo'ness and is not too pricey. Wall-days-only people can stop the night here; stroll the 3.5 km (2 miles) to Harbour Road after breakfast and have all the rest of the day for travel homewards. Full-Walk folk, doing the Extra Day, can also stop the night here; but do not worry about adding 5.5 km (3½ miles) to tomorrow's distance – I have a cheating option for you; see tomorrow's text!

Note:
This morning we head up through woods by a stream, the Polmont Burn, before entering Gray Buchanan Park. Today's route at first departs from the line of the Antonine Wall, but means we do not

have to walk along the M9 motorway, an activity frowned upon by law officers. We get refreshment opportunities in Polmont and Bo'ness (see text). After a final stretch of good Ditch in Polmont Woods and a stretch of woodland bridleway, we cross the River Avon to gain the line of the Wall overlooking the undeniably exciting Grangemouth oil-refinery and petro-chemical works. Kinneil Park leads us gently into Bo'ness. Our Trail down to the old part of Bo'ness; thence past the bus station, steam railway station, and along the shore, leads us to Harbour Road and the alleged end of the Wall by Bridgeness Tower.

There were two further supply forts: Cramond, where this Trail ends and with some foundations on view, and Inveresk, Musselburgh, beyond the scope of this study/trail (OK, it's too far!) If you choose the Richmond Park Hotel option, it makes tomorrow a bit long, so you can hop on a bus! More news, later.

Let's walk! Use the map.
If starting from Beancross (Travelodge or Metro Inn), go back through the pedestrian subway and turn left to a road junction where we cross the side road (on our right) *with care*. In 100m, *immediately* before a bus stop, turn right onto a footpath signed 'to Polmont Road'.

If starting from Cadgers Brae (Premier Inn), *return the way you entered – up the few steps – to the main road*. Turn left past the bus stop and left again onto a footpath signed 'to Polmont Road'.

Our footpath follows a stream (right) with the Brewers Fayre, Premier Inn, and a Garden Centre fenced-off to our left. Continuing up the tree-grown valley, we must, at the top of a series of steps, and just before a main road (A803) *take a left fork*. Our continuing path is seen directly across the road. Cross with care.

(1) The continuing path crosses grass and, descending, takes us across a bridge over a stream. Take the steps upwards (ignoring a path junction, left). At the top of the steps, our path bends sharply left, rising more gently. Behind us are increasingly distant views. The Antonine Wall is away below us. The Romans were trying to overlook the River Forth and did not require to be as high as we are. At the top, we turn left at a T-junction with the main drive through the Gray Buchanan Park. Soon we pass, right, the big house

Parkhill, now flatted. Stay on the wide main path, ignoring junctions. We pass a play park (left) before descending, gently, to the South Lodge at another road.

> (Note: **If you want Polmont Rail Station, go right on the road and keep your southerly direction for about 350m [yards].)**

Otherwise, turn *left* on the road which was an old country route which got built up and was superseded by a modern road (B810) which we soon see. Stay on the twisting old road: 'Marchmont Avenue': bear *left* at sign 'Marchmont Court' and go *ahead* into 'cul-de-sac' section. Turn right on Main Street, the A803 road.

(2) Soon we pass – or enter – the 'Black Bull', tel: 01324 716610. I can recommend (2012) dining here: go in the second door. *Or,* you may prefer one of the two take-aways further on. Cross the main road by turning left at the signalled pedestrian crossing and walk down a cul-de-sac side road at first called Greenpark Drive. You will note (right) the Claremont Inn, tel: 01324 719205. Continue: our road has become Airlie Drive with more shops, (right). At a T-junction ahead, turn right into Ashley Road and, at the end, take the footpath link to the main road. Cross with care and turn left. Cross the bridge over the M9 motorway and *immediately* on the far side, turn right (sign to 'Fishery') to walk down, parallel to the motorway. At the foot, go straight ahead through a gate onto a path leading into Polmont Woods.

(3) Beyond a 'kissing' type of barrier, at a path junction, curve left away from the M9. At a further path junction with a bench (ahead), *bear right* to go gently up a main path, passing another bench (on your right). This emerges on a tarmac path which we cross; and we go ahead and cross the wooden footbridge over Millhall Burn. Notice ahead of us, zig-zag steps up – with a metal hand rail. We go up these and turn right at the top. *Very soon*, we turn left up a straight steep flight of steps. At the top we are ON the Antonine Wall, where we go to our left. Soon, we bear right, where we find some steps leading downwards. Notice here the well-defined Ditch with berm on its south side. There is even a slight hump of Wall south of the berm. This is our last, reasonably spectacular, cross section of Wall. Go down the path/steps beyond

the Wall to a small car park. Cross this and *just before* the vehicle exit and a bridge, we turn right on a path signed 'Bridleway'.

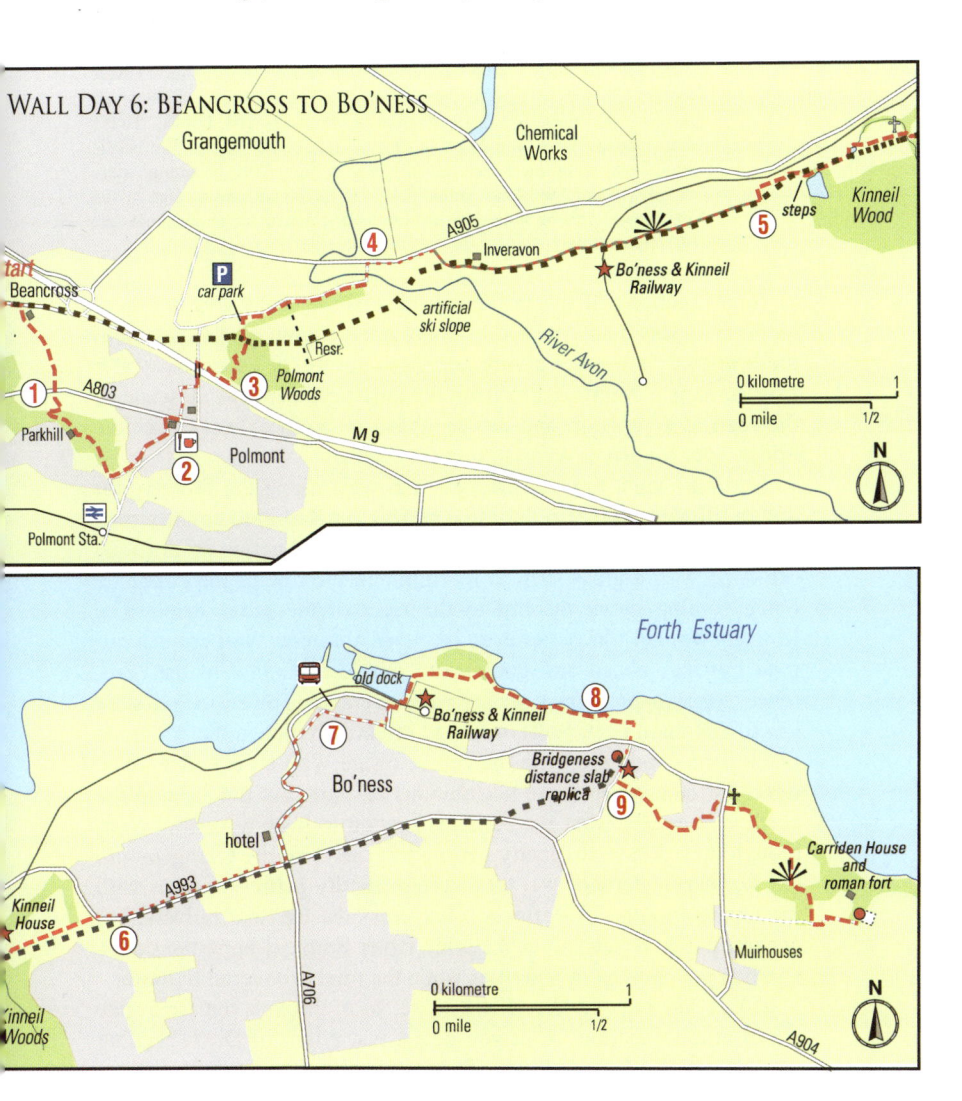

(Note: Some 300 m/yds. along the bridleway, our Trail is crossed by a public-right-of-way from the road [left] going to our right up a flight of steps. If you were *really keen* – and you should note that I am stopping short of actually recommending this – you *could* go up the steps then straight across a golf course fairway to go up a continuing flight of steps. At the top, the Wall approaches *on your left* before a fenced-in reservoir complex. It is *really* hard to detect any sort of Ditch, hollow, or whatever. *On your right* there is a cracked stone reservoir-associated wall. That's what happens when you build on top of a filled-in Ditch. The public right-of-way continues over the hill in a straight line, becoming more overgrown, and goes down to that fishery to which we saw the sign by the M9. Now, hurry back down to the bridleway, where our *un*-keen pals are patiently waiting.)

Some sections of the bridleway have stone walls and in places the Trail is less than 2 m wide. There are a couple of indications of the bridleway's use for giving access to points for collecting water from streams. Nearly 1 km from the small car park, we descend to the road at a junction and we go ahead to cross a 'weak' vehicle bridge over the River Avon to join the A905.

(4) Turn right towards Bo'ness and walk along the footway for 450 m till we turn first right into a narrow, unclassified country road. As we progress uphill and look to our right, we notice an artificial ski slope with a grass strip to its right and the line of the Antonine Ditch coming down the hill to the right of the grass strip. The Romans wouldn't have believed it! The Antonine Wall crosses *our* road by trees ahead and goes up to our left, parallel to the road; (check your maps). Once we are past Inveravon Tower, the possible site of a Roman Fort, (left), our road effectively lies in the Antonine Ditch for a good mile, with the course of the Wall on our immediate right. Roman remains are not obvious up here, but the view to the north is basically what the Romans needed to keep a lookout over, though they'd have difficulty getting to grips with the Grangemouth Oil Refinery. Perhaps we, too, have difficulty getting to grips with the Grangemouth Oil Refinery. We cross the Bo'ness railway, but generally enjoy views over the wide River Forth. I hope the tide is in when you arrive – it's prettier when the mud is covered by water.

(5) 1 km beyond the railway line, look through the field gate ahead at a T-junction. Can you detect just a hint of Ditch heading diagonally left of dead ahead? Turn left here (cycle route 76). After our route goes sharp right, look – in 200 m – for steps up to the right

and the *back* of a sign pointing towards them. (It is a Scottish Rights of Way and Access Society sign and says, on its front, 'Kinneil Wood, Bo'ness'.) Go up these 40 steps. The path is again on the line of the Antonine Wall. I think we are on the up-thrown diggings from the Ditch here. In the wood, bear left (route 76) to maintain our direction – noticing a pond on the right through the trees. At the end of the wood, go ahead down nine steps to grass. Pause here, before proceeding half right to Kinneil Roman Fortlet, marked out with an array of stubby square posts. I recommend checking the display board before walking north through the Fortlet and across the line of the Wall. Go ahead to a signpost by the edge of the wood, and then turn right, back on our Trail.

We continue, with the grass area on our right, towards a thicket which conceals a second pond. Bear left of the thicket and pond, following the path. Go left on leaving the pond and head over the grass area, with the vast bulk of Kinneil House ahead. Follow the path leading towards the house. The Antonine Wall is thought to have taken a straight line between Kinneil Fortlet and the right hand (south) side of Kinneil House. Can you imagine any traces of Wall or of Ditch? Soon we see a belfry (left a bit) on the gable of ruined Kinneil Church. Go and have a look. There was an entire medieval village on this site. Now we follow the path above the gorge of the Gil burn and cross it by the bridge. Across the bridge, we find a small cottage – now ruined – but used in the 1700s by James Watt for testing a stationary steam engine for pumping water from mines. Go ahead from the cottage to a gap in the wall by Kinneil House and follow the main drive away from the house. **There is a small museum (left) which is worth visiting (open 12.30-4.00, Mon-Sat, tel: 01506 778530).** The course of the Antonine Wall is now just over the masonry wall to the right of the main drive.

(6) Come straight out of the Kinneil Estate onto the main A993 road (bus route). Bear right on this main road which (after the curve straightens) runs in a straight line for 2 km because it is *on* the course of the Wall. You'll be disappointed when I tell you that *you are only going for 1 km*, because you must turn left at traffic signal controlled cross-roads to find the Richmond Park Hotel, 26 Linlithgow Road (EH51 0DN, tel: 01506 82321), across the road from Douglas Park (right). Some of you may be stopping here for the night, or perhaps you will eat here before continuing to Carriden.

The Trail continues down the road as it zig-zags down hill, (passing the Riverview Restaurant: for sale in January 2014. It's on your left in Church Wynd.) You eventually reach a traffic roundabout and turn right into Seaview Place, passing a chip shop (right, good chips!). Go ahead into North Street, passing Bo'ness Bus Station (in East Pier Street).

[Other eating places are: The Town Bistro (tel: 01506 829946) 17 South Street. Turn right at 'the Hippodrome Cinema' to find the Town Bistro at the end of this short street on your right. They open for lunch; also on Friday, Saturday, and Sunday evenings. Ivy Tea Room is at 68 South St (01506 823389). Bo'ness Blue, restaurant and take-away, is at 2 Main Street (opposite Commissioner St, see below) tel: 01506 829399.]

BRIDGENESS TOWER FROM BO'NESS STATION FOOTBRIDGE

(7) After seeing the bus station, we pass a 'Jubilee Drinking Fountain' (on the right side of the road). We pass the mouth of Commissioner Street (left), as our street becomes 'Main Street'. Our Trail turns left, opposite a shop 'Lidl', into Dock Street.

Presently, we find Bo'ness Steam Railway Station. It has a seasonal café, to go with its seasonal trains. In any event, our Trail crosses up-and-over Bo'ness Station footbridge; but pause on the top. Looking west, the old dock is in the foreground with Longannet Power Station beyond it, across the Forth. Looking south, the Antonine Wall ran along the ridge, with an excellent view north. If we look east, over the engine shed, we see Bridgeness Tower. The Wall's east end was about there. Now, we'll take the foreshore path – on 'reclaimed' land.

Walk past the end of the dock, passing the entrance to the Scottish Railway Exhibition. Past the dock, we bear right and take the main surfaced vehicle path which leads us between the River Forth (left) and an industrial area (right). We are on reclaimed land planted with groups of trees. If you find yourself going right towards houses, go left to follow the path nearer the shore. (This will make sense when you're there!) Soon we pass Upper Forth Boat Club's yard (right). Then we go *straight* through a gap in the wall ahead to continue on a concrete path by the shore. If you think this can be shut off if the water is rough – it can!

(8) At the other end, the concrete path goes up a ramp to a short railing. *Turn right to leave the shore.* Then curve left on the main track but, in about one minute, turn right to go along an alley to a barrier gate by the road. We cross the road and go up 'Harbour Road', opposite. Stop 150 m up to try to look at a stone slab on the right. This is an *old* replica of the original Roman 'distance slab' – the original being kept in Edinburgh. Walk uphill, crossing the mouth of Tower Gardens (right) and soon finding ourselves adjacent to a hedge. The Wall and Ditch are thought to have ended over the hedge, near Bridgeness Tower. We can look over a gate (right) to see a BOWLING GREEN. Many sections of Wall/Vallum have been flattened over the years and we have seen many of them, but this final section of the Antonine Wall clearly gets the prize for flatness. Did they do this *on purpose* just to be able to say: **"The Wall starts near Bowling, in the west; and ends at Bowling Green, in the east!"?**

Cross the road to the east side and stop at a map and information panels. Facing south, uphill, is a new (September, 2012) replica or 'facsimilie' (sic) – oh dear, oh dear, oh dear – of the original distance slab carved by the Romans around 142 or 3 AD. I think we may regard this new monument as marking the east end of the rather old Antonine Wall. (If you're heading off, now; bus no. 5 goes downhill to Bo'ness bus station; thence no. 45 to Linlithgow.) However, at least one authority – with justification which is not obvious to myself – believes the Antonine Wall continued to Carriden Roman Fort, a mile or so further. There seems no real archaeological evidence that the Wall did continue, but we can all agree the fort comprised a part of the Wall *system*. That is why this section goes to Carriden – not to mention the fact that Carriden House, on the site of the fort, offers up-market bed and breakfast.

(9) To continue to Carriden: just uphill of the distance slab monument, we turn left across the grass parkland keeping the ruined tower on your right and a group of mature trees on your left. As we pass these, we aim to the right of modern houses. (New and old Carriden Churches' steeples are seen, half left.) Do NOT yet access the housing scheme but pass to the right of the houses and follow the trodden way – with houses left and woodland right.

Avoid a tempting street access (left), but presently we are sort of led round leftwards on the grassy path to enter the housing area, passing a red dog poo bin and passing down between fences. Turn right on Kinacres Grove: (the back of the sign faces us). At a T-junction go right, uphill; soon to curve left and coming down to a vehicle turning circle. Here we take a footpath, half right, which goes between houses and brings us out across the road from Carriden Parish Church. Cross carefully, going smartly right and left to walk between gate posts onto a tarmac drive. When this drive turns back to the right, we go through a pedestrian gate on the left. Then ALMOST IMMEDIATELY turn right to head uphill.

Go past another gate to enter a field. Turn left along the field edge. After a few minutes, turn right at a path junction to go uphill *across the field* on a straight, grassy, path. See if you can spot a sign-post at the end of this strip, against the woodland. At the woodland *we turn left* at what that sign usefully calls 'path'. (Sorry, a minor touch of sarcasm escaped there.) Do admire the view northward from here. We go down 'path' through woodland to cross a footbridge over the Carriden Burn. Now, *turn right, uphill* (can be very muddy) to reach the Carriden House drive. We go left – though without doubling back – and soon our track curves left then right to pass 'The Steading' (left) then 'Carriden House' (also, left). This is the B&B. (Mrs Barbara Blackbourn; tel 01506 829811; web www.carridenhouse.co.uk). STOP at the edge of the field past the house and face the Firth of Forth. We are standing on the south boundary of Carriden Roman Fort near, or on, the point where the south gateway entered the ramparts. The east half of the Carriden House garden and the west portion of the field comprised the area of the fort. How are the mighty fallen! We can see no trace of the fort, but is the road on the line of the military way?

Oh: by the way, 'Kinneil' means 'the end of the Wall'!

THAT'S THE END OF OUR SIXTH, AND LAST, WALL DAY.
EXTRA ONE TO GO – IF YOU WISH.

THE GARDEN SHED SYNDROME

Note:
I have introduced this End-of-the-Wall topic to be read at the End-of-the-Wall part of the Trail. Our Extra Day offering, taking us along the coast to the site of Cramond Roman Fort, is in the next Section.

The Departure of the Romans from the Antonine Wall:
I referred, in PART ONE, to the departure of the Romans from Britain. Here we are going to discuss the departure of the Romans from their Antonine Wall.

Reading between the lines of some of the books which I have enjoyed, about the Roman occupation of Britain, I detect something of a paradox. Authors seem to express a *pride* in what the Romans achieved: one can feel a *fondness,* even, for those we seem almost to regard as having been our ancestors' fellow countrymen. Despite the fact that they conquered us, it is hard to find any word of deep hatred written about the Romans – nothing existing indeed like anti-Nazi or contra-Communist literature.

Is this not the greatest Roman achievement of them all? They tramped over (most of) our land: they defeated (most of) us: but we now admire them – *like them, even*!

Let us suppose we are living in 142 AD. Lollius Urbicus, under Antonine's direction, arrives with detachments from three legions to dig a Ditch and raise a Rampart right across our land. Outrage! We hate them! But surprise, surprise; soon the Romans are paying us money for our farm produce. We are in business. With this comes a sense of safety and security. Perhaps we get direct employment by the army, whom we knew had been in Britain for over a hundred and fifty years – some eight generations: security indeed!

But what have we now done wrong? After only twenty years – *one* generation – they get up and leave us!

Until modern times, historians have had difficulty explaining and dating our Roman past. In PART ONE I was a bit rough on the

[At Hopetoun Crossroads, no. 40 bus passengers go right, to find their bus stop. The route forms a loop, so you can board from *either* side of the road: buses going right – uphill (no. 40A) – are a little bit more direct. Downhill buses (40) – going to the left – pass Dalmeny Train Station, then go through Dalmeny Village. Both routes join the same dual carriageway (A90). Presently, towards the top of a rise, your bus leaves it again. *Think quickly here!* Over the hill, you pass a bus stop, but YOUR STOP FOR GETTING OFF IS ONLY 280m FURTHER, at a Miller and Carter Steakhouse at Cramond Brig, back on the main road. See Section 5, below.]

(3) Walkers: From Hopetoun Crossroads; go left – downhill – soon to pass where that diverted cycle route once joined our main road. Presently, having passed Queensferry Police Station (right), our Trail goes *ahead* at a road junction along the sett-paved Queensferry High Street. (Incidentally, the 'downhill' buses to Cramond Brig and Edinburgh City centre turn right at that junction to disappear up the steep hill.)

Section 4: Queensferry at west end of High Street to Cramond Brig: 9.5 km (5¾ miles)

As we wander along the High Street, you will have to decide whether to walk along the first-floor terraced route on the right or stay at ground level so you can nip down closes to see the sea. You'd be hard to please if you can't find refreshment stops along here. By the way, you'll find even more by the Rail Bridge at the end of the village where the Hawes Inn has some accommodation. (Public toilets are to be found near there – Ladies' on the right before the Hawes Inn, Gents' on the left beyond the slipway).

(4) Our Trail now follows part of Cycle Route 76 in the Dalmeny Estate. Just under the mighty Forth (rail) Bridge, bear left down a lane which leads to Longcraig Gate and the entrance to the Estate. We start by following the track of Cycle Route 76 – ignoring one or two side tracks. Included in 'things to look out for' are: Hound Point (left, see map) with great views and sandy beach; Barnbougle Castle (left, by shore), once the Dower House for Dalmeny. When our trail reaches a golf course with Dalmeny House ahead, we turn left to follow the shore path, on grass, by keeping the golf course on our right. We pass to the *left* of a wood. Then our path curves right to cross a stream by a footbridge. The

Section 3: Abercorn turn-off to Queensferry at west end of High Street: 6 km (3¾ miles)
You will recall, we were going straight on at that junction ([S] Queensferry 3½ Cycle Route 76). We follow a stream and arrive at a cross path where we turn left (Route 76). Hopetoun House is visible – side on (left). Presently our track becomes tarmac.

(2) We turn left at a T-junction just before rising ground (76). We are now heading east on a surprisingly well-surfaced private road which was once a scheduled bus route. At the top of a rise the Forth Road Bridge can, just, be seen. I can't answer for the new 'replacement' crossing since they have just (2012) started building it. Our route is deflected by a cottage then – as we pass, on our left, more 'Welcome to Hopetoun' signs – it resumes its former straight line but now as a grassy track. Go ahead, through a gate arrangement and proceed onward, ignoring a junction (left). Soon, at a T-junction, GO RIGHT – departing from cycle route 76 and the John Muir Way – but gaining views of the Forth Bridges. At the top of the rise, we bear left at an estate road junction and soon go through a gate at a lodge house, but keep walking ahead, past a gate and past 'The Banks'. Keep ahead here, now on a grassy path and going through a kissing gate. For a few hundred metres there are parallel paths. I prefer the left hand option: Bear left into a field and find an old stone paved way along the top (right) edge of the field, following a low wall (right). At the end of the field, bear right again – which joins the right hand parallel path. Soon, when we join an old tarmac path, we bear left and – at a junction – bear left to head downhill. Our informal road joins a public road at a kissing gate. On joining 'Linn Mill', bear left again. At the foot of the hill turn right on a more main road (Society Road). We have here rejoined Cycle Route 76 and, after we cross a bridge, our Trail and the cycle route did once fork left past a marina, but because of the Forth Replacement Crossing, now overhead, we now have to walk up the road, passing houses, to reach a main road at a junction known locally as Hopetoun Crossroads.

At this point our Trail touches another long distance walking route of mine: "The Saint Andrew's Way": a restored pilgrim route from central Edinburgh, across the River Forth, to St Andrews Cathedral. www.thesaintandrewsway.com.

Section 2: Blackness Castle to Abercorn turn-off: 3.5 km (2¼ miles)

Once over the footbridge, go through a gate into woodland (Cycle Route 76) and bear left to follow the main path, ignoring all turns, for 2.5 km (1½ miles), until the path curves left to cross the masonry Nethermill Bridge and then curves right, upstream – soon to arrive at a path junction: the 'Abercorn turn-off'. (The right arm heads up a series of zig-zags for ¼ mile to Abercorn Kirk, noted for interesting grave stones. It is ¼ mile back down!) *Our main Antonine Trail goes straight on* to South Queensferry (3½ miles). I have noted the astonishing wording on a padlocked, 2.4m (8 feet) high pedestrian gate at the junction, *with a roof to deter climbers*. Here goes:-

"Please note the land beyond this gate belongs to the Hopetoun House Preservation Trust and that access rights do not apply as outlined in section 2.11 page 12 of the Scottish Outdoor Access (sic) **Code.**

"An entry fee applies between Easter and the end of September. Outwith these times, the grounds are closed to the general public but . . ."

TREE ROOTS AT HOPETOUN

Beyond The Wall: Carriden to Cramond

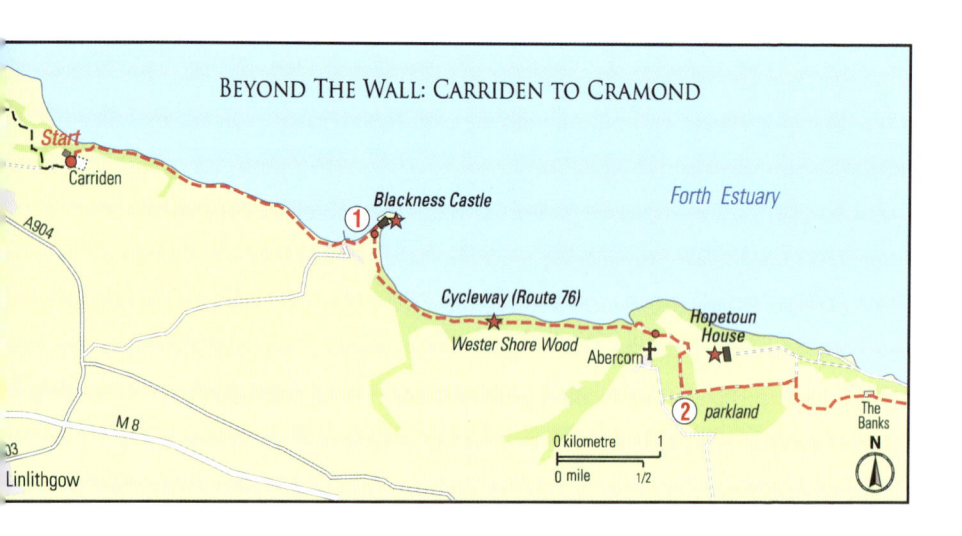

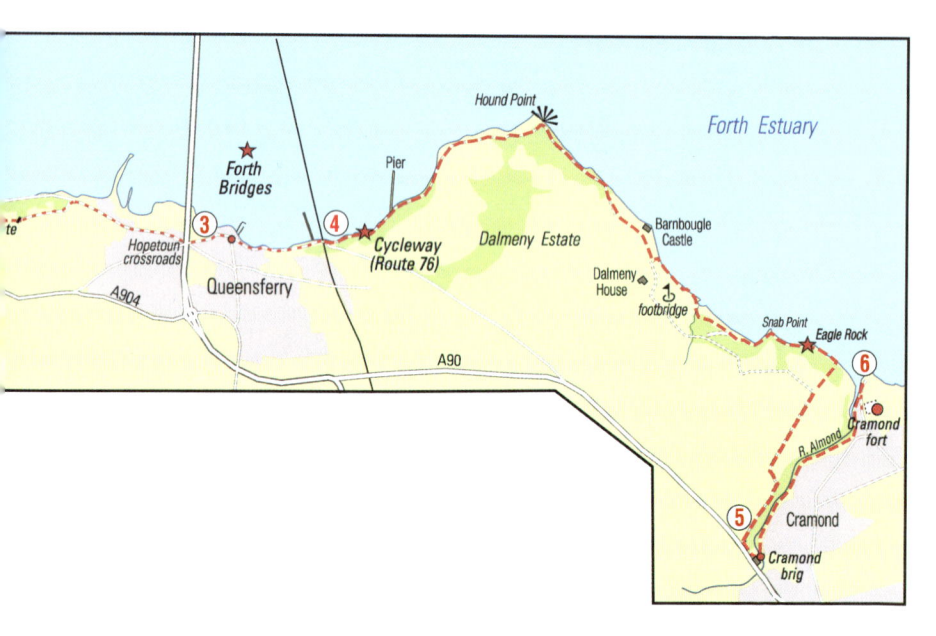

Let's walk! Use the map.

Section 1: Carriden to Blackness Castle: 3.5 km (2¼ miles)
(If, perchance, you are starting from Richmond Park Hotel, add some 5.5 km or 3½ miles to the distance. Then, cheating by using the 40 bus is recommended!)

From Carriden House, come out of the garden and turn left to the field. Our Trail turns *left again*, down the field edge towards the Forth. When our path leaves the field, we find another path, where we turn right. We also find a bench here. We go under a power line roughly at the north-west corner of the Roman Fort. Look at the views the Romans had! Our Trail is now on an old eastern drive from Carriden House down to the shore. Presently we join the shore path and go right towards Blackness – noticing, soon, that our 'drive' was heading for a gate-opening in the sea wall. We stay on the shore path. We are sharing our route with the John Muir Way.

At a cross fence, we are (2012) diverted to the top of the shore wall and presently, for a few metres, onto the sand. Path improvement work, doubtless inspired by John Muir, is in progress at the time of (re)writing (2014). Presently, we are on the seaward side of a 2 m high wall but on top of the sea defence wall. As we enter Blackness, we first pass houses (right) then an area where walkers park cars. Blackness Inn (right) was not open in 2014.

(1) Go ahead to Blackness Castle (Historic Scotland); it's included in today's mileage. After your visit, go round outside the south boundary wall of the castle to make your way above the beach to a burn, where you turn right until you can cross the burn by a footbridge.

(You *can* dodge the Castle: In the village, turn right uphill (Cycle Route 76 to 'Queensferry 5') along 'St Ninian's Way'. At the end of the road, follow the same line down a grass area, past a play-park, to the footbridge over the burn.)

EXTRA DAY: BEYOND THE WALL
CARRIDEN HOUSE (B&B) AND ROMAN FORT
TO CRAMOND ROMAN FORT: 25 km (15½ miles)

Here is the cheating option, I mentioned!

IF GETTING THE 40 BUS FROM THE WEST END OF QUEENSFERRY HIGH STREET TO CRAMOND BRIG, YOU WALK 15.5 km (9½ miles) – OR 21 km (13 miles) IF STARTING FROM RICHMOND PARK HOTEL

Note:
There is no opportunity (2013) of eating until Queensferry, other than coffee and ice cream at Blackness Castle. If you catch the 40 bus at Hopetoun Crossroads (just west of the 1964 Road Bridge) or in Hopetoun Road (opposite the police station, just before the west end of Queensferry High Street) you will miss Queensferry's eateries, but you could visit the 'Miller and Carter Steakhouse' at Cramond Brig *where you get off the bus* to walk down the right bank of the River Almond to Cramond. *Or:* you could wander through charming Queensferry finding several food outlets (Orocco Pier Hotel, on the left; and the Hawes Inn, almost below the rail bridge, both offer accommodation). Then, just past the Hawes Inn, steps, signposted, lead up to Dalmeny Train Station and that 40 bus route.

Today, we are following the south shore of the River Forth Estuary. A first section takes us to Blackness with its Castle (Historic Scotland). A second section takes us near to Abercorn Church. Next, we find ourselves in delightful Queensferry (refreshment opportunities). A walk through Dalmeny estate brings us to old Cramond Brig over the River Almond. Thence, down the riverside to Cramond Village, with Cramond Inn (food), Roman Fort, and buses to Edinburgh city centre.

The Garden Shed Syndrome:
I think we now have to consider the Garden Shed Syndrome. If you are old enough to have erected a Garden Shed at least 20 years ago, you may have noticed some maintenance requirements. The roof started leaking: perhaps you had to re-felt it. The door would not open/shut properly: perhaps you needed new hinges or had to correct the sagging joinery in some way. You allowed leaves and detritus to build up round the back: then you realised rot had set in and the rear corner was sagging and you wondered if you could afford a new shed. Perhaps a limb fell from your neighbour's tree and crushed your shed and you've had to live without it these last three years.

Whilst it would be unfair to describe Roman Buildings as Garden Sheds, they *were* mostly of wood, on stone foundations. (The Headquarters Building of each fort may have been stone: to protect the wages-fund and the Standard. Presumably wood was insufficiently robust.) They had put a lot of effort into the original rampart, ditch, and buildings construction, *within the memory of senior officers.* I would guess that many serious repairs or replacements were now required. Remember that natural consolidation had reduced the wall height; some ditches were silting up; some culverts were clogged and others collapsed; some bridges may have required attention.

One can imagine a management meeting on the Antonine Wall: "Well gentlemen, from these fabric-condition reports, we are reminded we have put off the major repairs but now a really intensive renewal programme is required. Luckily, Hadrian made us build in stone, down south, and the reports tell us these abandoned properties are generally in remarkably good repair. The civil populations on the Forth and Clyde estuaries and in the Borders area, between the Walls, seem peaceable. It would save on manpower and make economic sense to abandon the turf rampart, destroy the remains of the buildings, and move south to our original stone buildings – a bit warmer, too, I do believe!

"Any other business?"

So they went.

Venerable Bede. His predecessors really struggled with how many Walls crossed Britain, in what order they were built, and when, and by whom, and why. If you are following my plot – and even I am struggling – we were to discuss the departure of the Romans from the Antonine Wall. Just a few years ago, historians tended, it seemed to me rather to have *wanted* Romans to have remained here just a little bit longer. That is to say, some dated the Romans' departure a few or several years later than now believed.

Romans left evidence of their presence. They did *not* leave evidence of their absence: they merely stopped leaving evidence of their presence. The trick is to date the cessation. I see three fudge factors which render the trick tricky.

1) The innate desire, I have mentioned, to *hope* they had stayed a bit longer.

2) Inaccurate dating by earlier historians.

3) Phoney evidence: I posses a Roman coin. If I drop it at Castle Hill near Bearsden with a current coin of the realm and they are found, say 1,500 years in the future, would future archaeologists say "Romans were here till 2014 AD"? By our own time, a few Roman artefacts, dated after the now-believed Roman departure, seem to have stretched the period of occupation.

A Roman departure date after twenty years' occupation of the Wall may presuppose that Antonine himself authorised it. By having advanced north in 142 AD he had cocked a snook at Hadrian's earlier retrenchment policy. Now he could relax. Historians sometimes search for a reason for the abandonment in terms of manpower requirements elsewhere: trouble on the continent and/or down south could have shifted troops from the Wall.

However, *from 158 AD they prepared to reoccupy Hadrian's Wall*. Hadrian's abandoned stone forts were refurbished and reoccupied. If troops were required elsewhere, the 'urgency' seems to me to have been a touch tardy. And is there not one little problem? Hadrian's Wall was double the length. To man it with 'x' persons per kilometre required double the manpower of the equivalent Antonine Wall manpower. (You may remember we discussed this earlier, as it were, in reverse.)

path swings left to a headland (Snab Point). Just past this, on your left, *a large rock on the shore has a Roman Eagle carved on it by residents of Cramond Roman Fort.* If, to you, it looks more like Dracula in a cloak, this may explain the caution expressed on Historic Scotland's plaque. Soon, bear right, uphill to leave the shore behind you. Keep going ahead, your track soon becoming a tarmac road.

(5) Eventually, on emerging from the estate and going left, downhill on the public road, you will find yourself on ancient Cramond Brig (the Carter and Miller Steakhouse is to your right as you approach).

> (Time for a wee digression: By the time we all get to Cramond Brig, we shall have endured a 1.5 km (1 mile) boring stretch of track – heading *away* from the coast to get to a river crossing (2012) so we can go all the way down the other bank of the River Almond to get to the coast – Cramond. As I write, the Cramond folk are having a 24/7-footbridge versus part-time-ferry crisis. I should suppose that Edinburgh Council, who gave approval in principle – a year or two back – for the provision of a footbridge across the river Almond at Cramond, are delighted with the delay which is not of their making. And why is there a delay? Two local gentlemen have proposed a part-time chain ferry. This romantic means of crossing would need a fare to be paid and a ferryman: so it would be closed at night and at weekends and in the evening and in the winter unless a volunteer ferryman steps forward. Not – one might think – a user-friendly link in the Round-the-Forth Cycle Route. In the meantime, we better be alert for a river crossing at Cramond, and preferably a free, 24 hours a day, 7 days a week, one!)

Section 5: Cramond Brig to Cramond: 2.5 km (1½ miles)

(Those bus passengers, who got off at Cramond Brig, should make their way down behind the 'Miller and Carter Steakhouse' to the old Cramond Brig which crosses the River Almond. Here you may meet the walkers, whom I rather abandoned, standing on old Cramond Brig, waiting for the next Trail directions.) Complete the crossing of the old bridge – noting repair-dates carved on the right hand parapet – and, having passed a cottage garden (left), turn left into Dowie's Mill Lane which is the start of our exciting riverside path to Cramond. If, perchance, you have actually crossed directly by the proposed footbridge or red-herring chain-ferry, you'll miss the exciting river gorge but will have saved a couple of miles.

**EAGLE ROCK (telephoto shot) FROM CRAMOND PROMENADE
THE EAGLE IS NEAR TOP LEFT OF THE ROCK FACE**

(6) At Cramond village, we make our way up Cramond Glebe Road from the riverside houses and the moored boats (summertime). Almost at once we find a welcoming Cramond Inn – noting the Roman Centurion on the sign above the door. To visit Cramond Roman Fort, head uphill but turn first left then *immediately* right onto a path which takes us to the site. Here we find some excavated remains (gosh, stone!) and several useful interpretation panels. A first generation Fort is thought to have been Agricolan, c81 AD; second generation AD 142, courtesy of Antonine; the visible remains date from AD 208, the visit by Septimius Severus. Cramond Kirk is built on the site of the Roman basilica or headquarters building because it was an important site with a history. It also had a goodly supply of dressed stone! If you peer at the outside of the church you can find that some of the particularly large blocks have criss-cross diamond patterned grooves because that is how the Roman masons dressed the stone. The good folk of

Cramond are still crafty and I shall share some information about this that very few people still know.

CRAMOND INN SIGN

On our long walk along our Antonine Trail, actual earthen mounds surrounding forts have been in short supply (ditches yes;

mounds no): but Cramond has mounds. There's a simple explanation. They were put there by a bulldozer in the 1950s – I stood watching them do it! As I write, funds are being sought for a visitor centre and to re-excavate the bathhouse which was reburied, for safety, downhill of the fort. As with all but one of the Antonine Forts, no-one knows the Roman name for Cramond but at least this name has Roman antecedents. It comes from Caer Amon. The first word means fort – originally from Caere, a fortified town near Rome. The second word, like Avon, is derived from Latin *aqua* meaning water or river.

Thank you all for joining us. If you walked the entire distance, you covered 124.5 kilometres, that is 77 miles; but I believe I may have encouraged a little cheating. Nevertheless, you have completed this Antonine Trail and started to understand the ancient Roman mind-set. Congratulations! It remains for me to tell you how to get out of here. Walk up the short distance to the top of Cramond Glebe Road. You can follow a path, parallel to Cramond Glebe Road, which starts with the west wall of the church hall on your left and the Roman Fort on your right: You cross the rear car park and continue ahead, through two walled gardens (see picture on the next page); then you bear right to the main road – coming out onto the bus route near the top of Cramond Glebe Road. Buses to the city centre approach from your left and curve round to your right. The service number 41 bus stop is right across the road, the service is frequent and buses stop at The Mound, not far from Edinburgh Waverley Station, taking about, er, 41 minutes!

May I suggest that you may be interested in walking from central Edinburgh (St Giles' Cathedral) to St Andrews (Cathedral) following "The Saint Andrew's Way"?
www.thesaintandrewsway.com.

Thank you for embarking on this Antonine Wall Trail with us. Perhaps you will return to Edinburgh for another walking adventure!

**THE PATH HOME
THROUGH TWO WALLED GARDENS TO THE 41 BUS STOP**

ACCOMMODATION

I have divided 'An Antonine Trail' into daily sections with agreeable accommodation each evening. I tend to have had in mind groups of perhaps four to ten folk strolling together and desirous of remaining together for their overnight stops. If you are a single walker or are a pair or couple, you may well have greater flexibility and an ability to cover greater daily distances. The listings here are mostly on or close to the Trail and offer more flexibility. The wise walker will wish to plan carefully and book ahead. The lazy walker will want their luggage carried. All I can say is "Good luck!"

Lunch stops are mentioned in the text, each day.

This accommodation list offers more than two dozen places to stay – from which you may wish to select about four to seven. To help those of you who want to divide the Trail into distances to suit your own ability, I have added, to each Trail establishment, the cumulative distance in kilometres from the start of the Antonine Trail. This will enable you to plan your walk in fewer (or more) days. These are given in 'curly' brackets. Thus: {28.5 km}.

I have been surprised at how many changes have occurred while I have been preparing this book. I therefore advise you to check all details for yourselves.

Dumbarton
Positano B&B {0 km}   www.positano.org.uk
    OS Ref NS 403752   Tel 01389 731 943
    79 Glasgow Road, G82 1RE   (350m W of Dumbarton E Stn)
Abbotsford Hotel {2.5 km}   www.abbotsfordhotel.com
    OS Ref NS 413751   Tel 01389 733 304
    Stirling Road (A82), G82 2PJ   (400m from Trail: signposted)
Dumbuck House Hotel {3.5 km}   www.dumbuckhousehotel.com
    OS Ref NS 415745   Tel 01389 734 336
    Glasgow Rd (A814), G82 1EG   (300m & signposted from Trail)
Milton
Milton Inn {4.3 km}   www.miltoninn.co.uk
    OS Ref NS 424743   Tel 01389 761 401
    On A82, E of A814 jnct. G82 2TD (100m from Trail)

Milton (cont)
Travelodge {5.0 km}
   www.travelodge.co.uk/hotels/201/dumbarton-hotel
   OS Ref NS 429742   Tel 01389 765202 (Restaurant next door)
   On A82, south side, G82 2TZ   (On the Trail)
Duntocher
West Park Hotel {13.5 km}   www.westparkhotel1.com
   OS Ref NS 493724   Tel 01389 872 333
   On A82, north side, G81 6DB   (On the Trail)
Bearsden
Bearsden Premier Inn {25.0 km}
   www.premierinn.com/en/hotel/GLABUM/glasgow-bearsden
   OS Ref NS 553733   Tel 0141 942 5951 (+Burnbrae restaurant)
   278 Milngavie Road, G61 3DQ   (On Trail+restaurant next door)
Milngavie Premier Inn {25.6 km}
   www.premierinn.com/en/hotel/GLAWES/glasgow-milngavie
   OS Ref NS 554737   Tel 0871 527 8428
   103 Main St, G62 6JQ   (On Trail+Beefeater next door)
Kirkintilloch
Smith's Hotel {41.0 km}   www.smithshotel.com
   OS Ref NS 654740   Tel 0141 775 0398
   4 David Donnelly Pl, G66 1DD   (On the Trail)
Twechar
Twechar Farm B&B {47.0 km}
   OS Ref NS 699759   Tel 01236 823 216
   On B8023, near canal bridge, G65 9LH (100m from Trail)
Kilsyth
The Boathouse Pub and Restaurant with Rooms {50.0 km}
   Auchinstarry Marina   www.boathousekilsyth.com
   OS Ref NS 721767   Tel 01236 829 200
   On B802 at Marina, G65 9SG   (600m from Trail)
Castlecary
Castlecary House Hotel {57.0 km} www.castlecary.hotel
   OS Ref NS 786781   Tel 01324 840 233
   On B816, G68 0HD   (On the Trail)

Falkirk
Falkirk Central Premier Inn {71.5 km}
  www.premierinn.com/en/hotel/FALBEE/falkirk-central
  OS Ref NS 875802   Tel 0871 527 8388
  On A813, Camelon, FK1 4DS   (On Trail+Beefeater next door)
Hotel Cladhan {Off Trail}   www.hotelcladhan.co.uk
  OS Ref NS 891795   Tel 01324 627 421
  Kemper Avenue, FK1 1UF (*Alternative route avoiding tunnel*)
The Antonine Hotel {Off Trail}
  www.antoninehotel/falkirk.co.uk
  OS Ref NS 889799   Tel 01324 624 066
  1 Manor St, FK1 1NT   (*Off Trail*) Central Falkirk
  Suitable for a day or two's stay in town. Irresistible Name!
Beancross (M9, Junction 5)
Travelodge {83.5 km}
  www.travelodge.co.uk/hotels/349/falkirk-hotel
  OS Ref NS 925797   Tel 0871 984 6359
  W. Beancross Farm, FK2 0XS   (100m from Trail)
Metro Inn {83.5 km}
  www.metroinns.co.uk/hotels/falkirk
  OS Ref NS 925797   Tel 08450 555555
  Next to Travelodge, FK2 0XS   (100m from Trail)
Restaurants adjoining the above:
  Beancross Family Restaurant and Chianti Italian Restaurant
Cadger's Brae (300m beyond Beancross)
Falkirk East Premier Inn {83.7 km}
  www.premierinn.com/en/hotel/FALCAD/falkirk-east
  OS Ref NS 926795   Tel 0871 527 8392
  Cadger's Brae, FK2 0YS   (100m from Trail)
  Brewer's Fare Restaurant is next door
Bo'ness
Richmond Park Hotel {94.0 km}   www.richmondparkhotel.com
  OS Ref NS 996811   Tel 01506 823 213
  26 Linlithgow Rd, EH51 0DN   (On the Trail)
Carriden House (B&B) {99.5 km}   www.carridenhouse.co.uk
  OS Ref NT 025808   Tel 01506 829 811
  Carriden Brae, EH51 9SN   (On the Trail)

Blackness
Rosebank B&B {102.6 km}
    Tel 01506 834 373   (Slavin)
    OS Ref NT 052800   Beautiful garden! (slaving?)
    On B903, behind the Inn and north of the Church
    EH49 7WL   (100m from Trail)

Queensferry
Priory Lodge Guest Ho {112.5 km} www.queensferry.com
    OS Ref NT 129783   Tel 0131 331 4345
    8 The Loan, EH30 9NS   (100 m from Trail)
Orocco Pier Hotel {112.6 km}   www.oroccopier,co.uk
    OS Ref NT 130783   Tel 0870 118 1664
    17 High Street, EH30 9PP   (On the Trail)
Ravenous Beastie B&B {112.6 km} www.ravenousbeastie.co.uk
    OS Ref NT 130783   Tel 0131 319 1447
    15 West Terrace, EH30 9LL   (On the Trail)
    It is worth checking this web site for the poetry!
The Hawes Inn {113.4 km}
    www.innkeeperslodge.com/edinburgh-south-queensferry
    OS Ref NT 132805   Tel 01383 410 000
    7 Newhall's Road, EH30 9TA   (On the Trail)

Cramond
Cramond Mill (B&B) {123.6 km}   www.cramondmill.co.uk
    OS Ref NT 188765   Tel 0131 312 8408
    10 School Brae, EH4 6JN   (On the Trail)
    Located on riverside path. Mob: 07414732530

TRAIL BY TRAIN

'An Antonine Trail' is so well served by train stations that railway enthusiasts might wish to consider using commuting by rail to a lesser or greater extent, though purists may consider such thoughts to be out of keeping with the coast-to-coast walk idea. I shall list the train stations. How to make use of them, I leave to the reader.

Pre-Wall Day:	DUMBARTON EAST STATION	On Trail
	BOWLING STATION	150 m from Trail
Wall Day 1:	BOWLING STATION	150 m from Trail
	(KILPATRICK STATION)	Not recommended!
	DALMUIR STATION	1 km from Trail
	BEARSDEN STATION	On Trail
Wall Day 2:	MILNGAVIE STATION	0.7 km from Trail
	BISHOPBRIGGS STATION	1.8 km from Trail
	LENZIE STATION	2 km from Trail
Wall Day 3:	CROY STATION	1 km from Trail
Wall Day 4:	FALKIRK HIGH STATION	200 m from Trail
Wall Day 5:	POLMONT STATION	350 m from Trail
Wall Day 6:	LINLITHGOW STATION	By bus from Bo'ness
Extra Day:	DALMENY STATION	500 m from Trail
	EDINBURGH WAVERLEY STATION	By bus from Cramond

Notes: DUMBARTON EAST, BOWLING, KILPATRICK, & DALMUIR are served by trains from Glasgow Queen Street and from Edinburgh.
BEARSDEN & MILNGAVIE are served from Glasgow.
BISHOPBRIGGS, LENZIE, CROY, FALKIRK HIGH, POLMONT, & LINLITHGOW are on Glasgow to Edinburgh main line.
DALMENY STATION is served from Edinburgh.

Find ScotRail at: www.scotrail.co.uk
And Traveline at: www.travelinescotland.com

SOME SOURCE MATERIAL

Before writing 'An Antonine Trail' I re-read several volumes from this list, and some of them I read several times! I occasionally jotted down salient details, generally without source attribution; so – whilst I am not aware of having actually quoted anything directly – I must here acknowledge the excellent material available to me.

On history, Professor David Breeze stands supreme on the subject of Roman Frontiers, and he spearheaded the successful drive to have The Antonine Wall's obtaining World Heritage Site Status. Annes Robertson and Johnstone seemed keen that we should visit our Wall and I found their approach refreshing. Paul Carter's Guidebook to the Forth and Clyde Canal was informative as were my own four voyages along this waterway. Google maps quite suddenly included (some) footpaths on their satellite images, which was a help. John Davidson's Walks around Linlithgow were beneficial near Hopetoun. I have rather dotted around from one web site to another in a serendipitous way; discovering, for example, that Falkirk Historical Society had pioneered the charming route from Beancross via Parkhill's Gray Buchanan Park to Polmont which I found quite independently!

ROMAN HISTORY

David J Breeze. 'The Northern Frontiers of Roman Britain', Batsford, 1982&93
David J Breeze. 'The Antonine Wall – The North West Frontier . . .' RCAHMS, 2005
David J Breeze. 'The Antonine Wall', John Donald, 2006
David J Breeze. 'Edge of Empire. The Antonine Wall', Birlinn, 2008
Lawrence Keppie. 'The Antiquarian Rediscovery of the Antonine Wall', Society of Antiquaries of Scotland, Edinburgh, 2012
Alastair Moffat. 'The Wall, Rome's Greatest Frontier', Birlinn, 2008

Anne S Robertson. 'The Antonine Wall', Glasgow Archaeological Society, 1960
Anne Johnstone. 'The Wild Frontier, Exploring the Antonine Wall', Mowbray House Press, 1986
Robin Birley. 'Vindolanda's Roman Records', Roman Army Museum, 1994
Peter Jones. 'Veni Vidi Vici', Atlantic Books, 2013
Guy de la Bédoyère. 'Roman Britain', Thames & Hudson, 2013
Patricia Southern. 'Roman Britain', Amberley Publishing, 2013

CANALS AND WALKING/EXPLORING

Ian Finlay. 'The Lowlands', Batsford, 1967
Paul Carter. 'The Forth and Clyde Canal Guidebook', Strathkelvin, 1991
Guthrie Hutton. 'A Forth and Clyde Canalbum', Stenlake, 1991
(Map). Forth & Clyde and Union Canals, Geo Projects, undated.
Erl B Wilkie. 'Walking the Central Scottish Way', Mainstream Publishing, 1996
Hamish Brown. 'Exploring the Edinburgh to Glasgow Canals', Mercat Press, 1997&2006
Ian R. Mitchell. 'Walking through Scotland's History', NMS, 2001
Cameron Black. 'The Saint Andrew's Way', C Black, 2010
John Davidson. 'Walks around Linlithgow', Linlithgow Civic Trust, 2008

VARIOUS LEAFLETS, including:

Antonine Walks in North Lanarkshire
The Antonine Wall, Falkirk Council, et al.

NOTES